An Urn of Native Soil

by David Anderson

Printed in the United States of America

First Printing, 2014
ISBN 978-0-9860603-1-1

Country House Publishing Company
P.O. Box 29955
Austin, TX 78755

Book and cover design by Nancy McMillen

Wanderers outside the gates, in hollow
landscapes without memory, we carry
each of us an urn of native soil,
of not impalpable dust a double handful
anciently gathered—was it garden mold
or wood soil fresh with hemlock needles, pine
and princess pine, this little earth we bore
in silence, blindly over the frontier
— a parcel of the soil not wide enough
or firm enough to build a dwelling on,
or deep enough to dig a grave, but cool
and sweet enough to sink the nostrils in,
and find the smell of home, or in the ears,
rumors of home, like oceans in a shell. *

Malcolm Cowley

*"The Urn," from EXILE'S RETURN: A LITERARY ODYSSEY OF THE 1920s, by Malcolm Cowley, copyright 1934, 1935, 1941, 1951, renewed © 1962, 1963, 1969, 1979 by Malcolm Cowley. Used by permission of Viking Penguin, a division of Penguin Group (USA) LLC.

Acknowledgements

I thank the following persons for materials, memories, advice, and encouragement in this project: Cynthia Shoen, Hal Bruff, Sherry Bruff, Sir Basil Markesinis, Philip Bobbitt, Jim Hornfischer, Bea Ann Smith, Kathryn Lang, Joe Tetro, Liz Hilton, Jane Cohen, Harold Booth, Maxine Fickenscher, Jean Clymer, Patricia Eggenberger, Marjorie Berniclau Phillips Miller, Marilyn Catlett, Nancy Fisher, Elaine Peters, Ellen Kent, Walt Anderson, Joleen Hicken, Tania Culbertson, Ceil Cleveland, Jerry Footlick, Jerry G'Schwind, Hadley Barrett, Merrill Anderson, and Caitlyn Hubbard. I'm grateful also to some who helped but didn't live to see the book: Beulah Jantz, Keith Blackledge, and David Riesman. Thanks as well to the following, who supplied photos or illustrations: Patricia Eggenberger (p. 6), Maxine Fickenscher (pp. 11 and 12), Nancy Fisher (pp. 24, 36, and 160), Joe Tetro (p. 30), and Elaine Peters (p. 128).

Union School, the year after we moved
away. This teacher, Ms. Green, was my
seventh- and eighth-grade teacher.

[1]

On the Way to Everywhere

I have a tiny, yellowed clipping from a local newspaper, circa 1947. It reads:

PIE SOCIAL IS HELD AT SCHOOL

District 74 school, taught by Esther Atkinson, held a pie social Friday evening. Following a program made up of local talent, the pies were auctioned by Clarence Peterson. The clear profit of the auction was $105.80 and it will be used to purchase new library books and a cabinet.

For me, those three taut sentences evoke a rustic civilization as rich as Thomas Hardy's Wessex—and as extinct as Atlantis.

UNION SCHOOL was in the Platte Valley, 250 miles west of Omaha and about the same distance east of Denver. It was at the far end of Lincoln County, Nebraska, thirty-five miles from the county seat. The nearest paved road was eight miles away. Most of the roads were dirt—rich black dirt, like the adjoining fields—which could turn to ankle-deep mud if it rained enough. The county graveled only the roads that were on the mail route. The mail was our main link to the outside world: it brought our newspapers, letters from relatives (no one called long distance just to visit), baby chicks, seedlings, and occasional extravagances from the Montgomery Ward catalog.

We didn't feel isolated because we were on the way to everywhere.

The Union Pacific railroad and the great Lincoln Highway ran just across the river from us. They were three or four miles away as the crow flies, but we could see the trucks, tiny in the distance, and the smoke from the locomotives. When the wind was in the north we could hear the trains whistle. Knowing that they connected the east coast with the west coast assured us that we were in the middle of things.

We lived in a landscape constantly in motion. In summer the wind whips the grass into waves as restless as those of the ocean. The tiny purple blossoms of the alfalfa dance in place, and the bearded heads of wheat bend and sway like old men. The leaves of the cottonwoods quake in the light and the cotton from their seed pods floats dreamily through the air. Roadsides that appear brown and dormant turn out to be alive with grasshoppers erupting like popcorn in a hot skillet.

In winter everything on the plains tries to move south—great V's of ducks and geese high above, tumbleweeds rollicking across plowed fields, wisps of old snow and gravel blowing along the roads, dry stalks of sunflowers clicking against each other as they strain to break free and join the windy migration.

Paintings and photographs of the plains are always vaguely unsatisfying because they can't capture this ceaseless motion. However evocative they may be, they are inadequate for the same reason that a great picture of a running horse is no substitute for watching a horse run. The restlessness of the plains landscape is unsettling to some people, but to those of us born there it is as soothing as the surf is to a beach bum.

All the kids in the community went to Union School from kindergarten (which was called "beginners," probably to avoid using a foreign word) through eighth grade. It was a simple white frame box not much bigger than a one-car garage, with a steep gabled roof, a belfry, and four tall narrow windows on each side. Attached to the back was a lean-to that contained our heating fuel—one bin for corn cobs, one for coal. Built according to some standard plan for rural schoolhouses, it was as plain and functional as a granary. It sat on a flat one-acre plot of virgin sod in the middle of a flat valley six or seven miles wide. The nearest tree was half a mile away. There were ruts in the sod that some said were remnants of the Oregon Trail. Just outside the front door was a well with a hand pump, and in each rear corner of the schoolyard was an outhouse, one for boys and one for girls.

For over half a century the school was the heart of a community of twelve or fifteen families scattered over many square miles of plains. Some farmed the rich flat land of the valley, and others raised cattle in the rugged hills and canyons to the south. Some, like my family, did both. For all of us, Union community was our social world, safety net, workplace, entertainment, and education.

Esther Atkinson was the most revered of all the Union School teachers, at least during my time. She *looked* like a school teacher. She wore rimless glasses and had delicate features and thinning hair. Her stern face and confident voice conveyed the impression that no one had ever thought of disobeying her, and no one ever did. She drilled us relentlessly on multiplication tables and state capitals and verb tenses. In her mind, penmanship revealed the condition of the writer's soul, and improving the former was certain to benefit the latter.

Every day after lunch Mrs. Atkinson read to us. I don't remember what the books were, but I certainly remember the drama of her reading. By giving every character a distinctive voice and every scene a different timbre, she could hold the attention of fifteen kids ranging in age from five to fourteen. In her desk drawer she kept a hand-puppet, a monkey, which she used to entertain the younger children and to act out parables for the older ones.

One of our school's few visual aids was a device the British call an orrery, but which we called a planetarium. Through an assortment of sprockets and chains, a golf-ball sized earth rotated around a brass sun the size of a grapefruit. A marble-sized moon, half black and half white, rotated around the earth, mysteriously managing to always keep the same side toward the earth. Mrs. Atkinson insisted that we study the movements of this contraption until we were able to use it to explain the seasons and the phases of the moon.

"And this is just our little corner of the universe," she said. "There are millions of other suns, and other planets and moons orbiting around their own stars."

Mrs. Atkinson understood the educational value of a sense of wonder.

The pie social, held once or twice a year, was a major community event. Women baked fancy pies or cakes and men paid exorbitant prices for them to raise money for the school. The successful bidder won the right to eat the pie or cake with the woman who baked it, but wasn't supposed to know who that was until he unwrapped it—an interesting proposition, since most of the bakers and bidders would have been married. I was too young to notice, but there must have been some delicate etiquette to assure that (1) the bidding would be spirited, (2) the right husband would emerge as the eventual high bidder, and (3) the winner wouldn't think one of his bidding rivals was *really* a rival.

The auctioneer, Clarence Peterson, was a farmer in the neighborhood. He looked like he had stepped out of a Farmer Brown coloring book. He wore a hat with the brim turned down all around, a blue chambray work shirt, and bib overalls. He usually had a toothpick in his mouth, and when he wasn't working he parked his thumbs behind the shoulder straps of his overalls. His toes pointed in almost opposite directions. He loved to visit, but he didn't get much said because of his peculiar habit of speech. He filled all the pauses between his sentences with nonsense phrases, as auctioneers are wont to do, but Clarence did it all the time:

"I was a-startin' to cultivate the corn, an' that, an' so, an' then, by golly, it commenced to rain, come to see, b'gosh, an' that, so I sez to Mabel, I sez, can't do it now, doncha know, an' then, an' so, I give it up, an' then, by golly…" If you knew him, you didn't wait for him to pause, because he didn't. When you interrupted he stopped abruptly, almost as if he was grateful that you had eliminated the need for him to fill the space with words.

Clarence was always the auctioneer at pie socials, perhaps because there was never a pause in his speech, or maybe just because everybody liked him.

The report of the pie social was probably sent to the newspaper by Mrs. Atkinson. She kept the clipping for more than fifty years, and when she died her daughter Maxine gave it to me. Mrs. Atkinson would have been proud of the sum raised, and justly so. The price of a store-bought pie wasn't more than a dollar or two. There couldn't have been more than fifteen or twenty pies, and a hundred dollars was more than most of the bidders made in a month.

The program usually consisted of someone playing an accordion or a fiddle, women singing duets or trios, a barbershop quartet, and sometimes a man dressed up like Minnie Pearl, repeating her jokes and trying to make his falsetto sound like hers. The newspaper article's description of this as "talent" may be a bit extravagant, but it *is* talent if you don't know any better. The best singer in the community has the most beautiful voice in the world if you've never heard a better one, and the jokes your neighbor tells are hilarious if you've never heard any funnier. And even if they aren't as good as the performers you've heard on the radio, like Rosemary Clooney and Jack Benny, they are *live,* right there in the room with you.

PIE SOCIAL IS HELD AT SCHOOL

District 74 school, taught by Esther Atkinson, held a pie social Friday evening. Following a program made up of local talent, the pies were auctioned by Clarence Peterson. The clear profit of the auction was $105.80 and it will be used to purchase new library books and a cabinet.

Union School, painted by a
friend of Esther Atkinson.

[2]

Rustic Learning

M Y MOST VIVID MEMORIES OF UNION SCHOOL are of things like
the interscholastic horse-turd fight, pristine love in the alfalfa, and adapting the elegant geometry of Bud Wilkinson's split-T formation to a three-boy, three-girl football team. I remember little about
discovering the magic of reading or learning what a wonderful wide
world it is, but that must have happened too. For me and most of the
other bumpkins who carved its desktops with their jackknives, Union
School worked.

We didn't know how old Union School was. It was just there, and
had been throughout living memory. Some kids' parents, and possibly
even grandparents, had gone there. There were distant rumblings
from Lincoln about consolidating country schools, but it was hard to
imagine our community without the school.

Membership on the school board was passed around, and eventually most of the men served. The teacher was often a woman who lived
in the community. I've already mentioned everyone's favorite, Esther
Atkinson, wife of one local farmer and daughter of another. My first
teacher was Jean Gustafson, daughter of a farmer who lived a couple
of miles from the school. She had attended Union School herself only a
few years earlier. Like most rural teachers, her preparation consisted
of a few "normal training classes" in high school and maybe a summer
at Kearney State Teachers' College.

Miss Gustafson was blonde and fair, wore pinafores and starched
blouses with puffy shoulders, and had a wide smile and the shy sweet
disposition of an angel. She was gentle and motherly with me and the
other younger children. I gathered that some of the parents had been

apprehensive about having so young a teacher, but by the end of the
year she had won over the entire community. She also won the heart
of a young farmer, Lou Clymer. She married him, quit teaching for a
while, and had children who also attended Union.

I loved all my teachers at Union, some as mothers and mentors,
some in other ways. My next-to-last year at Union we had another
young teacher, Ilene Johnson. She was only five or six years older than
I, and when the wind pinned her thin cotton dress around her legs I
had strange and exciting sensations. In my prepubescent confusion I
could only express my lust by tormenting her—mimicking her behind
her back in the schoolroom, snatching her headscarf during recess to
expose her hair to the mercy of the wind.

Teaching all the grades in one room may have been a nightmare
for the teacher, but for the students it worked pretty well. Usually
there were only one or two pupils in each class, so it was a little like
having a private tutor. When it was time for third-grade reading, say,
the third-graders sat on a bench at the front of the room and took turns
reading aloud. The rest of us stayed at our desks and worked on our
assignments or listened to the class at the front. Those who were a little
behind could listen to lessons they should have learned in the lower
grades, and those who were quick could learn from the higher grades.
My sister Ellen recalls that teachers sometimes had older children help
the younger ones with their assignments. I was usually the only kid in
my grade at Union so I learned at my own pace. I learned so much from
listening to the older kids that when I was supposed to start the second
grade, the teacher decided I should skip ahead to the third.

Troublemakers had plenty of opportunity to snicker at the mis-
takes of the younger kids or pester a neighbor while the teacher was
busy, but teachers quickly learned to solve that problem by giving the
miscreant more work. We were all given a lot to do, and we learned to
concentrate on our own work despite the distraction of the class that
was reciting. We learned without constant attention from the teacher.

Field trips were homegrown. Jerry G'Schwind recalls that the
whole school hiked several miles into the south hills to see the wreck-
age of a plane that had crashed there. For another schoolmate, Maxine

Atkinson (now Fickenscher), the most memorable outing was when the teacher allowed the older girls to go to my house to see my newborn sister, Ellen.

Somehow the teachers found time to teach us music, art, and poetry as well as arithmetic, geography, penmanship, spelling, and grammar. We sang "Little Joe the Wrangler," "Red River Valley," and "My Old Kentucky Home," and we had a rhythm band. I remember memorizing Rudyard Kipling's "If" and Alfred Tennyson's "Crossing the Bar."

It surprises me now to realize that people whose lives had so little room for luxuries valued these amenities even though they lacked any practical utility. Like most others in the community, my parents had not attended college, played no musical instruments, and quoted no one more poetic than Will Rogers. But they wanted their children to know music and art as well as arithmetic and grammar.

Mrs. Smith, the wife of our mail carrier, taught piano in her home in Brady. Although I had no talent whatever, my parents insisted that I take lessons. Mother would fetch me from the field and insist that I sit down for a few hurried minutes of practice before she drove me to Mrs. Smith's for my weekly lesson.

When it became obvious that I was never going to learn piano, I was given the option of switching to classical guitar, but not of quitting altogether. Mrs. Smith tried for a year or so to teach me to play the guitar, but that didn't take either. Only when my sisters got old enough to replace me in my parents' ambitions was I allowed to lapse into the musical illiteracy for which I was cut out.

The school had no library, of course, but there was a county lending library that circulated books to all the rural schools in Lincoln County. A traveling librarian came about once a month from North Platte and brought ten or twelve books for all the grades. About the third grade I discovered the liberation of reading, and I was soon devouring all the books in the first week or two. From then on my teachers and the librarian conspired to supply extra books for me and my friend Joe Tetro, who was also a voracious reader.

I read the popular children's series, such as the Hardy boys and the Bobbsey twins, but my favorites were books like *Smoky the Cow*

Horse by Will James and Andy Adams's *Life of a Cowboy*. They depicted a life I knew something about, and one I dreamed of living.

The pupils all had responsibilities. The most coveted job was ringing the bell; the lucky kid got to come early and start ringing exactly thirty minutes before school started. You could keep pulling the bell rope until your arms wore out or the noise got on the teacher's nerves. Hoisting the flag in the morning and lowering it at the end of the day was another choice assignment, but one that could be a challenge with the wind blowing thirty miles an hour.

Some of the kids lived three miles from school, but we lived only a little more than a mile away. We walked to school unless someone happened along and gave us a ride. Usually the passerby would be a neighbor, but I didn't decline a ride even if it was a stranger. I don't recall ever being warned to beware of strangers; they were assumed to be people just like us, and therefore not to be feared. If any parent worried about kidnappers or child molesters, I never heard of it. Today I hear rumors that there may have been child abuse in one family, but at the time such possibilities didn't trouble our parents' minds.

Halfway between our place and the school the road crossed the Tri-County Canal, a deep ditch that carried a lot of Platte River water to a series of reservoirs in the hills south of the valley. The bridge was wooden, ten or fifteen feet above the water and forty or fifty feet long. The surface consisted of planks laid crosswise to the road. Periodically the county closed the bridge to replace worn or broken planks, usually just a few at a time. There was another way to cross the canal but it required a long detour, so usually I just jumped across the gaps where the planks had been removed. Once, however, the county removed all the planks at once, leaving in place only the beams that ran the length of the bridge. The current was swift and I couldn't swim. I was detouring around until Joe Tetro dared me to walk across on one of the beams. It wasn't more than six inches wide, and if I had fallen I would have drowned, but I made it across.

There was no point in walking across the canal on a beam except the risk itself, and I deserved a whipping. I didn't get one, because the only eyewitness other than Joe was my ever-loyal little sister Elaine, who watched in terror but didn't tell on me. That's the only totally senseless risk I remember taking; the others were incidental to some activity that had a point.

On the very nastiest days our parents drove us, by tractor if the roads were impassable by car. In the great blizzard of 1949, snowdrifts ten feet deep closed the roads for two weeks. School was closed for the first week, but the second week Dad hauled my sisters and me to school in a livestock trailer pulled by a tractor, avoiding the drifts by driving across fields and pastures where the wind had cleared the snow. He tied a tarp around the stock rack to block the wind, and at first it was a great adventure, but the bone-jarring ride across rough frozen ground became a dreaded ordeal long before the drifts melted.

That great storm gave us a new form of amusement, or rather a variation on an old one. Most years the late fall winds drove hundreds of tumbleweeds into the barbed-wire fences on the north and west sides of the school yard. When the wind let up, we gathered tumbleweeds, which we stacked and packed to make walls and forts. The road ditches were always full of sunflowers, and when those dried in the fall their stalks were like bamboo poles. We laid them across the tumbleweed walls and by piling more tumbleweeds on top we made tunnels and clubhouses.

The storm of 1949 gave us a new building material: The snow that winter was so deep and lingered so long that we were able to carve out big blocks of hard snow, which we used as building blocks instead of the tumbleweeds. Our igloo-style tunnels and rooms were cozier and classier than those made of tumbleweeds, but nature never again furnished the right kind of snow. Usually our snow seemed more like dry ice—it came down in flaky dry crystals that wouldn't stick together and seemed to be capable of evaporating without leaving a trace. Unless we got enough wet snow for a snowball fight or a game of fox and geese, we had only the usual schoolyard games—ante-ante-over, crack-the-whip, 23-skidoo.

The six-man football team in the
Union schoolyard, 1951. "Our team
included three girls; the other boys in
school were too little to play."

[3]

Love and Combat

I FIRST FELL IN LOVE AT UNION SCHOOL. When I was in first grade, the cutest girl ever to skip through the sandburs at Union School started as a beginner. Her name was Elizabeth Strobel. All the boys liked her, but I was the most ardent. I colored little squares of paper cut from my Chief tablet and wrote "I love you" on every page (not realizing, of course, that she couldn't read). I bound the pages together into little booklets, and I gave her a booklet every day for several weeks. Finally I had to stop because her mother complained to the teacher that a lecherous seven-year-old had designs on her five-year-old princess.

But Liz liked me too, and love defies suppression at any age. I continued to woo her until the end of the year, when we had an end-of-school picnic in a grove of trees half a mile from the school. The grove had once surrounded a farmstead, but the buildings had long since been removed. In that shady and romantic spot many initials had been carved in trees—eons ago in child time, probably five or ten years in adult time. The wind in the trees made mysterious noises. Earth, weeds, decaying logs, mushrooms, and new leaves collaborated to create the heartbreaking smells of spring.

I doubt that Liz appreciated the endlessness of summer yet, but I did, and I knew that I wouldn't see her much until school started again. I don't know if we knew about kissing then; if we did it probably seemed silly. But some nameless primordial need made me want desperately to hug her and hold her. I couldn't do it at the picnic because other kids and the teacher were always around. The other kids would have humiliated us with their teasing, and the teacher would have instantly put a stop to our amour, probably by swatting me on the bottom. But after the picnic opportunity knocked—or rather, waved in the wind. We walked back to school through a field of alfalfa as high as our chests, thick and in bloom, ready to be cut. I took Liz's hand, we lagged behind the others for a bit, and then we dropped to the ground, completely hidden from anyone more than a few feet away.

We lay in the fragrant uncut hay for a while, exchanging "I love you's." Maybe we hugged each other, maybe not; the memory lodged in my brain is of immaculate love unsullied by corporeal existence.

When we got up and began running toward the school, we discovered that we had dallied too long. Our absence had been noticed. A worried teacher and a bunch of merciless, smirking kids had started back through the alfalfa looking for us. The teacher was so horrified that she even scolded Liz. As for me, she thought expulsion was the appropriate penalty. She threatened to report me to the school board and I believe she would have, but the year was over and the board probably didn't meet again until fall. I like to think that by then the teacher had developed a more charitable attitude toward love. In any event, I never heard any more about it.

All community activities were organized around the school even if they weren't school-related. The 4-H club for our community was the Union 4-H Club and the one from the next school district east was the Pleasant Valley 4-H Club. Once, somebody decided we should have a joint meeting to stimulate friendship and cooperation between the two clubs. But the murderous concept of "us" and "them" was already lurking in our juvenile psyches, and we were soon engaged in a snowball fight, Union vs. Pleasant Valley. We were meeting at the Tetro ranch, which was in our territory, but the visiting Pleasant Valley kids had us trapped inside the horse corral. They were on the outside where they had the protection of the fence and some mangers, and we had no cover. Both sides were firing as fast as we could make snowballs.

Then someone on our side made a discovery of the kind that alters the course of warfare. On the ground inside the corral were small piles of horse turds, nice and round like baseballs, covered with snow, and frozen solid. The gods of war had supplied us with readymade ammunition, right where the horses left it. Now we didn't have to waste time making snowballs; we just grabbed the nearest horse turd and fired away. When one hit a board it sounded like a rifle shot. When one hit a kid it made a satisfying thud instead of the soft "poof" of a snowball.

We had the Pleasant Valley kids pinned down behind their cover and were advancing on them to demand their humiliating surrender, when some little kid got hit in the head with one of our miracle missiles and began screaming as if he had been shot. The adults came running, the Pleasant Valley kids cried foul, our 4-H leader apologized to theirs, and our parents raised hell with us. That was the last joint meeting of the Union and Pleasant Valley 4-H clubs.

I said we had no sports. That's not quite true. My last year, when I was in eighth grade, we had a football team. It grew out of the first book I ever owned, *Oklahoma Split-T Football,* by the great coach Bud Wilkinson. It described a revolutionary new theory of football. In the split-T, the linemen lined up about a yard apart, instead of shoulder-to-shoulder as they did in the single-wing formation or the ordinary T-formation. That spread out the defense and sometimes gave the offensive linemen an angle on the opponents they were supposed to block. The split-T opened up the game and paved the way for many of the standbys of modern football, such as trap blocks. The book contained many diagrams showing how the O's could neatly obliterate the X's from various criss-crossing angles. I was taken with the logical beauty of these ideas and was eager to try them out.

The only available players were my schoolmates, and they weren't eager to be my pawns just so I could try out Bud Wilkinson's theories. So I proposed that we field a team and challenge the Pleasant Valley school to a game. That idea would have appealed to our competitive instincts anyway, but it was especially attractive in the aftermath of the horse-turd fight. Neither school had enough kids to field an eleven-man team, so we played six-man football as they did at Brady High School. Our "six men" included three girls; the other boys in school were too little to play. We practiced for weeks, but since we had no one to scrimmage against, our workouts were like shadow boxing: We blocked imaginary defenders and eluded ghost tacklers.

Game day was a community occasion. We played on their territory, but parents from both sides came and we each had our own cheering section. We played tackle football, but the contact wasn't exactly ferocious, since we had no helmets or pads and had not been able to practice blocking and tackling against real opponents. A lot of touchdowns were scored, and at the end there was some confusion about the score. The parents decided to call it a tie, which infuriated our team because we were sure we had won. The Pleasant Valley team was content with the tie, which proved to us that they were sissies, even worse than town kids.

I wonder now whether Union School was as educating and re-inforcing for everyone as it was for me. My family and our friends were insiders. Most of us had been born in the Union community and started and finished grade school there. Our fathers rotated on and off the school board and our mothers were pillars of the Ladies' Aid Society. What was it like for the children of transient farm workers, who attended Union School for a few months or a year or two, often starting and leaving in mid-term, arriving with different school experiences and later trying to transport whatever they learned at Union to yet another school? I suppose we seemed smug and exclusionary, and I know we were sometimes cruel. I remember once hitting or pushing a girl on the school ground. Her father, a hired man, happened to be working in the adjoining field. He stopped his tractor, rushed over to the fence, and warned me to never mistreat his daughter again. I was shamed to the bone.

A few of our neighbors were desperately poor, like the family that lived for a few months in a dugout in a hillside in the Sytsma canyon, more than two miles from school. They had six children, including a boy who was crippled from polio and hobbled to school dragging one leg in an iron brace. Another family, motherless, lived in a tarpaper shack; the eldest girl attended school in addition to keeping house for her father and two or three younger children. We made fun of the ragged, patched, or ill-fitting clothes the poor kids wore and the odd foods they brought in their lunch boxes.

But sustained snobbery requires an excess of people, and that we never had. The girl I pushed could run fast and we needed her on our football team. The boy who had had polio was such a game competitor despite his shriveled leg that he was always taken early when we chose up sides for games, and we coveted the little cars and trucks he carved from sticks and gave to his friends. We recognized that the girl who took care of her father and siblings was stronger and better than the rest of us, even if her clothes didn't fit.

I'm sure some of my schoolmates have memories of Union School that aren't as rosy as mine. There are probably slights that still rankle, humiliations that still hurt, educational failures that can't be repaired. But I doubt that Union inflicted any more of those than kids in our circumstances would have suffered in any other school, and at least we were all spared the ultimate indignity: nobody at Union School was ever ignored.

*"Our houses were pretty much
surrounded by corrals, barns,
and sheds. You learned to watch
your step as soon as you learned
to walk." Above: Nancy and me
with a newborn calf, circa 1943.*

[4]

Rural Realities

W HEN THE ROADS WEREN'T IMPASSABLE, we went to town on the
day the stores stayed open late—Brady on Thursdays or Gothenburg on Saturdays. Gothenburg was a little farther away but bigger.
North Platte, the county seat, was thirty-five miles away; we went there
only on special occasions, maybe three or four times a year.

Brady was a ranch town, squeezed into a narrow spot between the
river and the sandhills to the north. It provided supplies and entertainment for a few large ranches and many smaller ones. One of Brady's
two grocery stores was known as "Grubby's," not as a commentary on
its hygiene but because grub was what it sold. Brady had three beer
joints, while Gothenburg, with ten times the population, had only one.
One of the Brady beer joints operated punch boards, which were the
poor relations of slot machines. You paid a nickel or a dime to punch a
tiny slip of paper out of one of many holes in the board; if you punched
out the lucky slip you won the jackpot. I suppose it was illegal gambling,
but the law was a long way away.

In summer the Brady merchants paid someone to show movies
of Hopalong Cassidy and the Durango Kid in the vacant lot between
the grocery store and the drug store. We sat on planks and the picture
was projected onto the side of Edwards Drug Store. It was here that I
encountered my first foreigner, at the age of five or six. A tiny Mexican
boy, younger than I, was pretending to stab other kids sitting in the front
row. I was terrified because I had heard grown-ups say that Mexicans
carried knives and could skin a man alive without making a sound.

Gothenburg was a farm town, which gave it a more settled and
respectable culture. It had eight or ten churches, a policeman, lots of

merchants, and a real movie theater. You couldn't play a punch board there. There were substantial houses with lawns on shaded streets, and a few of its streets were paved.

Whether you went to Brady or Gothenburg, you spoke to everyone you met, and if you knew them you stopped for a chat. On shopping day, there were clusters of people visiting all up and down Main Street. A trip to town to buy a few groceries and a roll of barbed wire could easily take three hours, but you always returned with news.

Lest my description of our lives conjure visions of *Little House on the Prairie,* there are certain realities I must acknowledge. Such as flies and manure. I first learned to distrust Hollywood because of its inability to deal with these truths. Watching the westerns on the side of the drug store in Brady, my friends and I guffawed at the implausibility of the scenes. When Gene Autry sang to his Sweetheart of the Rockies, no fly ever dared alight on her palpitating bosom, no matter how many fly-attracting animals were nearby. Or eight horses standing at a hitching rack, and nary a horse turd in sight; did the movie-makers hire squadrons of nimble men with shovels to dart onto the set and remove the droppings before we could notice them?

I once saw a play in Sydney that opened with a scene in a country graveyard. While waiting for the preacher to arrive so they could bury their relative, the family members discussed what might happen, now that the last family member willing to live on the ancestral land had died. Their conversation was punctuated with desultory variations on fly-swatting: the vague flick of the hand at a fly that only made a reconnaissance pass, the vigorous two-handed execution of one that moved too slow, the quick brush-off of one that landed on an ear. To the Australians, who know that the fly is the most persistent fact of life in the bush, and to we Americans who knew life on the plains, those gestures conveyed instant authenticity, just as surely as their absence from Hollywood's westerns signaled fake.

The main economic activity of our community was the raising of livestock, and the principal product of livestock is manure. Our houses were pretty much surrounded by corrals, barns, and sheds. You learned to watch your step as soon as you learned to walk. As a young child, one of my earliest fascinations with nature was watching dung beetles work. They rolled marble-sized balls of manure and buried them in the ground to nourish their larvae. We called them tumblebugs, because they stood on their front legs and rolled the ball with their hind legs, and when the ball got big they sometimes tumbled into a somersault, landing on their feet and going right back to work on the ball.

For every pitchfork of hay or bucket of grain you fed to a cow or horse, you could count on having to remove a roughly equivalent amount of manure. What fell in the corrals was left to disintegrate on its own, but what fell in the barns had to be carried out to the manure pile. We had special manure forks, wider than pitchforks, for that purpose. As winter progressed, the hay stack on one side of the barn got smaller and the manure pile on the other side got taller. In spring we loaded the manure into a wagon equipped with a mechanism that spread it evenly on the fields as fertilizer.

The weather was often terrible. On average, the temperature in that part of the plains is below zero on sixteen days of the year and above ninety on forty days. The average annual precipitation is twenty inches, barely enough to sustain agriculture. One day in the early '50s, the official temperature in Gothenburg reached a hundred and sixteen. In 1947 a tornado hit just east of our farm. It tore the roof off the home of our neighbors, the Baileys, and leveled a swath of trees through the river bottoms all the way to Gothenburg. Lightning occasionally killed a horse or cow, and we sometimes lost crops to hailstorms.

The only thing predictable was wind. Except on a few miserably sultry summer days, there was always a wind. Sometimes it blew twenty to thirty miles an hour all day. We never knew exactly how much snow had fallen, because the wind blew it off the open spaces and piled it up in deep drifts on the downwind side of buildings and windbreaks. I haven't found official statistics on wind velocity, but when I asked a friend who lived there fifty years, he said, "Fifteen miles an hour would be about normal. When it gets up to twenty or twenty-five, people would say it's getting a little windy."

We had coyotes, skunks, and rattlesnakes. Many nights we could hear coyotes howling somewhere in the distance, and occasionally they killed a newborn calf. (Today I understand that coyotes rarely kill a calf, so maybe they just eviscerated one that had died naturally.) Skunks loved eggs; if we heard a commotion at night in the chicken house, Dad took down the 12-gauge shotgun that rested on two nails above the kitchen door, had one of us kids bring a lantern or flashlight, and tried to maneuver the skunk into the open before shooting it. Shooting a skunk in a building was a big mistake, one you would smell for weeks.

Rattlesnakes were more common in the hills, where we pastured our cattle, than in the valley. When I was five, Dad left me to look for some fencing staples while he walked a pasture in the hills looking for a sick cow. In a dark shed I spotted a tall coffee can that looked like it might contain staples. As I reached for it, a rattlesnake lying coiled beside it suddenly buzzed. I ran from the shed screaming, "Snake! Snake!"

Dad was barely visible on a distant high ridge, but he heard me and came running. He thought I had been bitten; I suppose he assumed that if I hadn't been, I would have just killed the snake and told him about it later. When he realized I was okay, he found a rusty sickle, killed the snake, and gave me the rattles, which I still have.

The amount of space and expense people now lavish on their bathrooms will always seem peculiar to those of us who came of age in the outhouse era. Hardly anyone I knew had indoor plumbing. At school, at church, and visiting neighbors or relatives, we all availed ourselves of the standard two-holer. To say outhouses had charm would overstate the case, but they did have character. They were made of wood, and after a few years in the weather the boards warped and cracked and the door sagged. On sunny days you could sit inside and watch dust motes dance in the thin sheets of light that sliced through the semi-darkness. In winter you could expect to find about as much snow on the seat and floor as there was on the ground outside. The cracks of course meant that the flies had unimpeded ingress and egress, and kids could spy on each other, though most lost interest in such unremarkable matters by the time they were four or five.

For obvious reasons the outhouse had to be twenty or thirty yards from the house. On days of mud, snow, cold, or rain, the trip was not a welcome one. A walkway, consisting of wide boards laid end to end, led to our outhouse, but the boards quickly warped, split, or slid out of place. On winter mornings when the boards were covered with frost, we learned to step as lightly as Peter Pan. Night trips were always to be dreaded. For the round of bedtime trips, a kerosene lantern was lighted and each of us carried it in turn. But if you had a call later in the night, you could only hope there was enough moonlight to find the walkway, and even if there was, inside the outhouse you would have only what moonlight found its way through the cracks. Nights are chilly on the plains on all but the hottest summer days, and most of the year they range from shivering-cold to frostbite-cold. The wind makes ghostly shrieks and blows phantom snakes against your hurrying legs. I expect that anthropologists will someday discover that bladder capacity of humans peaked just before the advent of indoor plumbing.

Ken Tetro, circa 1930, wearing the
chaps Joe Tetro gave me 75 years later.

[5]

Ambiguous Feelings

W HEN I WAS BORN, my parents were new to the community and
had no money, but Doc Pyle accepted the promise of a calf in
the fall in lieu of a fee for delivering me. My father was working as a
forty-dollar-a-month hired hand on the ranch of Kenneth and Dorothy
Tetro. The Tetros provided a four-room house, a half-gallon of milk
a day from the cows Dad milked, and a share of the meat when he
butchered a hog or a dry cow. My mother helped Dorothy with laundry,
house cleaning, and children. My parents had whatever vegetables my
mother could grow in a small garden beside the house (fresh for a few
short weeks in summer, canned for the rest of the year), chokecherries
and wild plums that Mother picked in the canyons in summer, and
pheasant, duck, or goose when Dad was able to shoot one.

Within a year or two, with Ken's help, we were able to rent a 160-acre
farm in the valley and buy a 200-acre pasture in the hills. My family was
soon immersed in the life of the Union community. In underpopulated
places, everyone matters, and newcomers are welcome. Whenever a
new family moved into the community, we and our neighbors called
on them within a few days and then exchanged intelligence with each
other about the newcomers' children, their possessions, from whence
they came, and the reason for their move.

The Tetro name was no doubt French, but on the principle that
foreign pronunciations were un-American, everyone pronounced it
TEE-tro. The Tetros tried to call the ranch "the Lazy 8"—their brand
was a figure eight lying on its side—but the name didn't stick. People
considered it pretentious to call your place a ranch, let alone give it a
name, unless it was really big. So, like its more modest neighbors, it

was simply called by its owner's name—"the Tetro place."

The Tetros were a little different from the rest of us. They counted among their friends some "rich people" from town, Doc Pyle and the pharmacist, Paul Potter. We thought Ken had inherited the place from his parents and therefore wasn't struggling to make mortgage or rent payments like the rest of us, but I've learned that was not so. The Tetros were buying the place from his father and lived in fear of losing it, just as the rest of us did.

The main thing that set the Tetros apart was that they weren't frugal. They drove a Buick, and later a Cadillac. Ken kept fine horses just because he liked them. He was a good calf roper, and in summer when everyone else was working fifteen hours a day, he occasionally traveled to rodeos pulling a horse trailer behind his fancy car.

Ken was a severe-looking man, of slight build, with narrow shoulders, thin wrists and small hands. He wore rimless glasses and had a thin face and a prominent Adam's apple. He didn't look the part of a rancher or roper, but he was wiry and tough. He had a mean temper, which I saw him unleash once on a horse. He had bought a flashy registered quarter horse colt that he called Blackie, and he was trying to teach Blackie to work cattle in a corral. Blackie was rearing and throwing his head back, so Ken got a short piece of a tree branch, as thick as his wrist, and whacked Blackie mercilessly over the head every time he reared. I remember him later saying, "The way to break a horse of that is to take a bottle of wine and break it over his head. When he feels the wine running down he thinks it's his blood."

Ken had an airplane, a single-engine two-seater that he kept in a shed at the ranch. He took off and landed in a field of rye. Ken used the plane in the summer to check on cattle and windmills. Flying over pastures that were back in the hills far from roads, he made sure the windmills were pumping water and kept tabs on the movements of the cattle and the quality of the grass.

In winter he used the plane to hunt coyotes. He removed the door on the passenger side and my father or someone else sat in that seat with a shotgun. A neighbor named Carl Strobel had a pack of hounds. After a snow, Carl would turn the hounds loose in a pasture while Ken and the hunter circled overhead. When the hounds got up a coyote, Ken brought the plane down low so the hunter could blast the coyote with the shotgun. It was dangerous sport; they were flying over rugged hills and canyons, and they had to fly low because shotgun range isn't more than forty or fifty yards.

That daredevil streak was another thing that set Ken apart. I've heard he had a favorite entertainment for his passengers. Flying a few hundred feet above the Tri-County canal, he would say, "See the muskrat swimming down there?" When the passenger said, "No, I don't see it," Ken would nose the plane down, dive into the channel (which was only a little wider than the wingspan of the airplane), level out just above the water, and ask the terrified passenger, "Now do you see it?"

I had my first plane ride with Ken when I was seven or eight. He must have done some stunts, because what I remember is the ground, dotted with miniature cattle, spinning in circles directly in front of us.

His flying career ended with a disastrous crash. He was checking windmills and noticed one not working right. He tried to land the plane on a grassy ridge near the windmill, but either the plane stalled or a downdraft pulled him nose-first into a small canyon of the sort we called a pocket. He had a back injury and bad cuts around the head and face, but he was far from any road or habitation, so he walked back to the ranch, three or four miles away. He was in the hospital a week or two. His was the wreck we hiked to see on our "field trip" from school.

We owed a great deal to Ken Tetro; he helped us escape from being hired hands. After we had worked for him a year or two, a neighbor died unexpectedly and his widow offered to rent us their farm for three hundred dollars a year. Dad went to the bank in Brady and tried to borrow the money but was turned down. The widow was poised to rent her farm to someone else the next day. Mother and Dad went to the Tetros and asked their help. Ken agreed to go to the bank with Dad the next morning.

Ken and the banker went in a back room for a while and when they came out the banker said Ken had agreed to co-sign Dad's note. Dad refused to take the loan on those terms. His maternal grandfather in Sweden had lost the family fortune by co-signing a note for someone, and the lesson had impressed itself on Dad so deeply that he wanted nothing to do with a co-signed note, even as beneficiary. The banker talked privately with Ken for a while, and then agreed to make the loan without Ken's signature. Obviously, however, it was Ken's endorsement that changed the banker's answer from "no" to "yes." Over the next year, Ken helped out further by lending us machinery and paying Dad for occasional work at the Tetros' place.

Mother always had warm and grateful feelings toward Ken Tetro, but Dad didn't. He acknowledged the debt we owed Ken, but harbored no affection for him. Dad had little appreciation for people who spent the family's money on expensive playthings and amusements for themselves.

More important, Dad thought Ken mistreated Dorothy. In later years he told me Ken had been a womanizer. I don't know if this was true or if Dad just assumed that anyone who would indulge himself with airplanes and expensive horses, or go off rodeoing when there was work to be done at home, was probably indulging himself with women too.

Dorothy was a small, nervous woman. She was the kind of woman Dad always admired—refined, dependent, and deferential. Once, many years after the event, Dad told me of a conversation he had with Dorothy, an encounter that probably left them both conflicted. It took place one evening while Dad was working for the Tetros, when Ken was away. After Dad had finished milking the cows and running the milk through the hand-cranked separator to draw off the cream, Dorothy asked him to come into the house.

"Arnold, I just don't know what to do," she said. "I'm just so unhappy."

The immediate source of her unhappiness was Ken's parents, Fred and Stella. Although they lived an hour away in North Platte, they apparently kept close tabs on the ranch and Ken and Dorothy and their children. Dorothy said she didn't feel like the house was her house and was never sure whether Ken's first allegiance was to her or his parents.

"I just wish we could just get away from here and leave all this behind," Dorothy said.

When I asked whether she meant her and Ken, Dad replied indignantly, "Well, sure. She meant they needed to get away from Ken's folks."

Still, the boss's wife confiding her unhappiness to the hired man, also married, would have been a large step outside the boundaries for both of them. As far as I know that breach of convention was never repeated, but I suspect it had a long afterlife. It unleashed a protective impulse in Dad, one the rules didn't allow him to obey. Any mistreatment of her by Ken, real or imagined, would have fueled his frustration and his anger toward Ken.

When Dorothy committed suicide twenty years later, I don't recall that anyone blamed Ken. Her emotional instability by then was well known, and assigning blame had not assumed the importance that it has today. But as many years passed, and perhaps as he came to understand more about human interdependence, I think Dad began to fault Ken.

Ken came to my mother's funeral. Dad accepted his sympathies, correctly but without the warmth you would expect in a friendship that went back fifty years. He never talked to Ken again.

"The closest thing we had to household help was a neighborhood spinster named Cora Jacox. Cora was a tiny, frail creature, lonely no doubt, but unfailingly cheerful." Above: Me, circa 1942, in front of the Jacox barn.

[6]

Characters

THE NEIGHBORS MY PARENTS WERE CLOSEST TO were total oppo-
sites of the Tetros. If the Tetros had more flash and dash than the
rest of the community, Clarence and Mabel Peterson had even less.

I've already described Clarence, the perennial auctioneer at pie
socials. Mabel was one of those legions of women who doggedly insisted on bringing bits of civilization to the plains. She looked like a
nineteenth-century pioneer woman, and she crocheted, made quilts,
and embroidered samplers for the wall. She had a tall, mahogany-
colored pipe organ with ebony knobs and ivory keys that was the pride
of their household. In later years she rarely played anymore; I suppose
she lacked occasion to play, got rusty, and lost interest.

She was the organizer of the women's book club, and I would guess
there were meetings at which she was the only woman who had read
the book. Spring, summer and fall, there were always flowers growing
against the foundations of their house, and somehow she managed
to keep a little patch of lawn alive in front of the house. Those were
heroic accomplishments, because the Petersons had no fence around
the house to protect the flowers and the lawn from the depredations of
their chickens, ducks, and geese.

The Petersons had two sons who were grown, or nearly so, by the
time I knew them. The youngest one, Bob, told me the first dirty joke I
ever heard: A sailor arrived in port and met a girl. He didn't have a rubber
so he used a handkerchief. A few years later the sailor returned to the
same port. He saw a scrawny little kid, all twisted and deformed. "Kid,
what happened to you?" the sailor asked. The kid said, "What do you
think you'd look like if you'd been strained through a handkerchief?"

I wasn't more than six or seven, but I understood the joke—or possibly I understood it after Bob explained it to me.

Clarence loved to fish. The Tri-County irrigation canal ran between our place and theirs, and on summer evenings Clarence often sat on the bank with a cane pole, the brim of his straw hat turned down all around as it always was, his shirt soaked with the sweat of the day's work, one thumb hooked in the suspender of his bib overalls. Occasionally he caught a crappie, more often a couple of bullheads. Even if he caught nothing, he seemed content to let the heat of the day lift while he watched the bobber pull his line tight against the swift current.

The Petersons rented the quarter-section across the road west from ours. They were the people my parents asked to do our chores if we were going to be away overnight, and the neighbors they left us kids with if they needed to go to a funeral or go to the hospital to have a baby. Clarence and Mabel were finally able to buy a farm of their own, but it was late in life, after they should have been retired, and it was a hardscrabble dryland farm on the table land fifty miles away from the Union community where they had reared their children and made their friends. I suppose that while they were trying to accumulate enough money to buy, the price of valley land escalated out of their reach. My parents continued to visit them occasionally, but it wasn't like having them half a mile away. I visited them once after I was grown. They seemed cheerful but it was obvious they were lonely and displaced.

My parents were also good friends with Johnny and Dorothy G'Schwind, who rented a farm a few miles away. One or two evenings a month, my parents played cards, pinochle usually, with John and Dorothy. The G'Schwinds had a son, Jerry, a little younger than I, and a daughter Patty, the age of my sister, Nancy. The four of us, plus my younger sisters Elaine and Ellen, were left to entertain ourselves. In summer we played hide and seek in Dorothy's rows of eggplant. In winter Jerry and I did experiments with his chemistry set and didn't concern ourselves with what the girls were doing.

Johnny came from Custer County, which was also my mother's home, and as young people they had dated. Johnny was a happy-go-lucky man, lanky and loose, with a rakish mustache. Dorothy was a schoolteacher type, serious and bespectacled. I had the feeling Dad thought Mother appreciated Johnny's fun-loving personality a little too much. Johnny didn't take farming too seriously, and Dad faulted him for that. But they all loved to play cards. They were quiet and intent while playing but when each hand ended the room was full of laughter and banter as they reprised the hand.

The closest thing we had to household help was a neighborhood spinster named Cora Jacox. Cora was a tiny, frail creature, lonely no doubt, but unfailingly cheerful. She took care of us when our mother was in the hospital giving birth to our younger siblings, helped out for a few days after Mother came home, and stayed with us on rare occasions when our parents were away overnight. I suppose we paid her a little, but she was really like family. She didn't drive, so sometimes she called and asked us to bring her something from town. Often we took her to town with us. We took meat to her when we butchered a cow or a pig, and she often sent a pie home with us. When she fell and broke an arm, she called us and we took her to the doctor. She called on us when she needed us, and we called her when we needed her.

The community had its eccentrics. An elderly woman known as Grandma Coleman lived with her son and his family less than a mile from us. I dreaded being sent there on an errand. Grandma Coleman had totally white hair, hollow cheeks, few teeth, and vacant eyes. Usually she sat silently in a chair in the kitchen. If she was in her chair when I arrived, I considered myself lucky; if she wasn't, that meant she was likely to appear unexpectedly, like an apparition. She seemed to be able to move soundlessly. If I was talking to the Colemans, I would be startled to realize that she had come to a doorway—or had she been there all along?

Going to other rooms in the house was the worst. We might open a door and there would be Grandma Coleman, perfectly still, staring. If she spoke, she made no sense. She might say "Kill a chicken for dinner" with dinner already on the table, or "Too much snow" in July. People said she was harmless, but she seemed like a witch to me. Some people said she was crazy. Others said "no, not crazy, just senile." I suppose she had Alzheimer's, though I don't think any of us had heard that term.

There was a man I knew only as Crazy Ed, who lived in a tarpaper shack on the road to Brady. He seemed to spend most of his time walking the road. He always dressed in black and wore a tall black hat and overcoat even in summer. He was so skinny he seemed like a skeleton inside his heavy clothes. He had enormously long legs and seemed to be very old. His gait was unpredictable; he might seem to be shuffling along, and then lurch toward the middle of the road just as we passed him, or take a great long stride toward the ditch. If we had had more imagination, we surely would have called him Death.

Less eccentric and more exotic was Dick Craig, who impersonated Buffalo Bill. Dick lived up the canyon where we pastured our cattle, but much farther back in the hills. He was a sober, hard-working, thrifty rancher who raised Hereford cattle and often did business with my father. He was no different from his neighbors except that he looked like Buffalo Bill.

"I started to let my whiskers and hair grow one winter when we were snowed in," he told a reporter many years later. "Just decided I wouldn't shave till I could get to town."

By the time the snow finally melted, he liked his new look and everyone said he looked just like William F. Cody. So for years Dick wore his reddish hair shoulder length, cultivated a goatee and mustache, and flared the brim of his hat upward on one side in the dashing style Cody made famous. He had a handsome gray horse with a stylish step, and a fancy silver-mounted saddle and bridle. He rode in the parade at every rodeo, town festival, and Fourth of July celebration in the area.

When Dick got too old to ride, another rancher from the opposite end of the county, Charlie Evans, took on the role. Evans made a career of it and became a more famous Cody impersonator than Dick ever was. But for my generation, Buffalo Bill was Dick Craig—not Charlie Evans, maybe not even William F. Cody.

Most of our entertainment was homemade. My favorite was the shivaree, an ancient ritual for welcoming newlyweds to the community. The idea was to wait until the couple had gone to bed and presumably were doing what they were newly licensed to do, and then surprise them. At the first shivaree I remember, we all drove with our lights out, then parked along the road a quarter-mile from the newlyweds' house. The men brought shotguns, the women carried pots and pans, and some of the older kids had firecrackers.

While we waited in the darkness for the last light to go out in the house, a few of the men passed around a bottle. People visited quietly and shushed the children. I shivered, and I'm not sure whether it was from the chill or the excitement. When the lights finally went out, we waited a few minutes longer, then crept up to the house, congregating under windows, especially what we thought to be the bedroom window. When somebody fired a shot into the air, all the other shotguns let loose, the firecrackers went off, and the women clanged the pots and pans together.

The noise didn't stop until the half-dressed bridegroom came to the door and invited everybody in. Inside, the bride, wearing a robe and slippers no doubt acquired for this very occasion, blushed dutifully, and everybody congratulated the couple. The groom handed out cigars to the men and candy to the kids, and the bride served cookies or cake. One or two men made mildly bawdy remarks, which they no doubt blamed on the whiskey when their wives scolded them on the way home.

There's no telling how many couples' sex lives got off to a bad start from the distraction of listening with one ear for the shivaree.

Occasionally a traveling salesman came through, selling lightning rods or vacuum cleaners or encyclopedias. They were as welcome as a sudden rain shower on a hot afternoon. People rarely refused to invite the salesman in, and his looks, speech, dress, wares, sales pitch, and success in the neighborhood would be a subject of discussion for the next week.

The most successful salesman I recall was one who sold "automatic fire extinguishers." They were sealed glass globes about the size of a softball, containing a colored liquid and mounted on a bracket on the wall or ceiling. The theory was that if a fire broke out in the room, the heat would break the globe and the special fire-extinguishing liquid (the name carbon tetrachloride lurks in my memory) would put out the fire.

No one could resist the promise that for a dollar or two your loved ones and your possessions could be protected even if you were asleep or away. Before that man left, every house in the community had two or three blue or red globes. Eventually I suppose someone found out whether the liquid would actually put out a fire, but by then the salesman was long gone.

The 1940s were good times for the plains and for Union. My family grew and prospered. Within a dozen years, my parents had four more children, owned a thousand acres of land, and were well-known breeders of registered Hereford cattle.

When my family moved away in 1952 to be closer to high school, the Union Ladies' Aid Society gave my mother a quilt. Each member embroidered a panel with a flower and her signature. Somebody then sewed the panels together and assembled the whole into a quilt. I've since learned that these were called "friendship quilts." The women of Ladies' Aid made no attempt to coordinate colors or styles or scale, but the quilt is all the more lovely for that—thirty individual visions melded by fellowship into a work of art and affection. My mother made one of the panels herself; I suspect they had her make one so she could participate in the project without realizing it was for her.

The panels of that quilt are like a roll call of the community. Mabel Peterson, the emissary of culture, is there. So is Ruth Scott, who played the piano for every soloist at every talent show and for every Christmas carol at every school program. My beloved first teacher, Jean Gustafson Clymer, is there, and so is Stella Tetro, Dorothy's dreaded mother-in-law. Edith Craig, sister-in-law of our generation's Buffalo Bill, is there, along with Dorothy G'Schwind and three Colemans—one of them must be the Grandma Coleman who filled me with terror, and the others wives of her son and grandson.

I sometimes wonder if they had an inkling, as they embroidered and gossiped and laughed, that their world was about to vanish—that the quilt they were making would soon be a treasured relic of a lost way of life.

*The panel Mother embroidered for
the Ladies' Aid Society quilt. "The
panels of that quilt are like a roll call
of the community."*

Our house and barn at Maywood.
"We were drawn to Maywood by the
same thing that drew our ancestors to
Nebraska: the lure of cheap land."

[7]

Misery and Malingering

THE FEW UNHAPPY MEMORIES I have from childhood are mostly from a brief time we spent away from Union. We moved to a place forty miles away, near Maywood, a nice little town with its own strong sense of community. But if you live in the country you're never really part of the town community. And there was no rural community for us at Maywood, perhaps because we lived only two miles from town, or maybe because population on the table land where we lived was too sparse to make the critical mass that community requires.

For me, the twelve years we lived at Union are like a pleasant dream, gauzy and imprecise, in which only happy incidents stand out boldly. The eight months we lived at Maywood are more like a nightmare, in which every frightening scene replays itself, more intensely each time, and no detail is lost.

We were drawn to Maywood by the same thing that drew our ancestors to Nebraska: the lure of cheap land. We were renting our farm in the Platte Valley, and the ambition of every farmer is to own his land. Dad did some scouting and found out that land was a good deal cheaper away from the valley. The hills south of the valley are no good for farming, but if you keep going up the canyons you eventually reach a high, broad plateau between the Platte River to the north and the Republican River to the south.

The table land isn't as flat or fertile as the valley land, and at that time it wasn't irrigated, as valley land was. It was dryland wheat and cattle country, and that suited Dad fine. He was interested in raising cattle, not crops, and he could convert the wheat fields to hay. In 1947 he bought the place near Maywood, half farm land and half pasture.

The first purchase was only four hundred acres, but over the next year or so he bought several adjoining places and eventually assembled a nice ranch of almost a thousand acres.

There was a reason, of course, why land was cheaper at Maywood. In the valley farms were well kept. Buildings were painted and in good repair. As you drove up the canyons away from the valley, buildings began to look shabby. Houses were often unpainted, barns sometimes in such disrepair that they were propped up with poles angled against the sides. Some farmsteads were abandoned. As you came out of the canyons onto the table, things improved a little. There were some well kept farmsteads, but they were set in a vast treeless landscape, so far apart you sometimes couldn't see from one to the next. Compared to the valley, it seemed unsettled, lacking the rudiments of civilization.

Maywood was forty miles from the nearest paved road. It was a town of about three hundred, hidden below the table in the narrow valley of Medicine Creek, a pretty little stream that meandered through the hills for fifty miles before emptying into the Republican River. At Maywood the creek was dammed to form what was said to have been a lovely reservoir, but in the spring of 1947 a flood washed it out. All that remained of the lake when we moved there were mud flats.

We moved to the Maywood place between Christmas and New Year's 1947. The ground was covered with old snow when we made the long drive in our 1941 Ford sedan out of the valley, up the canyons, and finally up onto the table. We arrived in the last bleak light of a midwinter day. To reach our place we drove two miles north from Maywood on U.S. Highway 83, which ran from Mexico to Canada but was still just a gravel road across Nebraska. We turned off the highway and up a hill onto a track through the grass, and followed that for three-fourths of a mile across the pastures, through two barbed wire gates. All we saw at first as we climbed the hill was the top of a windmill. Then the top of a huge red barn came into view, and finally a one-story frame house. They were on the highest point around, and except for one scrawny cedar tree a quarter of a mile away, there wasn't a tree in sight. It seemed like you could see to the North Pole, and the wind felt like it had just left there.

In a book called *The Indian War of 1864,* a cavalry officer named Eugene F. Ware described an Indian-hunting expedition that ended with a long ride up the Medicine Creek in January 1865, probably across the land that became ours:

> *Riding against the wind was very unpleasant; all of us had our heads muffled up in the capes of our overcoats, and we kept our roadway by peering through openings in the folds of our capes. As we were riding against the wind we would look out through our capes with one eye. In a little while the tears of that eye would be frozen up, and vision entirely obscured; then we would shift our capes to the other eye while we warmed up with our hands and thawed the ice from the other eye.*

When the detachment got back to Fort McPherson on the Platte Valley, every man had suffered frostbite, and the general who led the expedition asked to be sent back to the war against the Confederacy, telling Ware that "he had lots rather go down South and be shot to death than stay up North and fight Indians and be frozen to death."

Eighty years later, winter on that section of the plains hadn't softened.

From our house, only one other farmstead was within sight, two or three miles away on an equally high point. Our house had no electricity and no plumbing. Telephone service was theoretical; there was a wooden crank phone on the wall and we were on a party line owned by the ranchers, but the line was often down and even when it wasn't, the static generally made it impossible to hear. To make a call we usually went to the telephone office in town, where you told the operator who you wanted to talk to and watched her plug in red rubber-covered wires to make the connection.

We were accustomed to trotting to the outhouse; there was no indoor toilet at our house in the valley either. But that house did have running water and reliable telephone service, and most important, it had electricity. The REA hadn't reached our place at Maywood. We used kerosene lamps at first, but those were smoky and put out little more light than a candle, so Dad bought a state-of-the art gas lamp that put out about as much light as today's fuel-burning camp lanterns. It sat in the middle of the dining room table and we all spent the entire evening around that table. Anyone who doubts that electric lights are the most significant advance in modern history hasn't lived a winter without them.

A coal-burning stove heated the kitchen and dining room—people believed it was neither necessary nor healthy to heat bedrooms. In the valley, our bedrooms were on the second floor so they received some heat from below. But at Maywood, they were in a wing of the house completely closed off from the heat and exposed to the merciless north wind. We kept chamber pots in the bedrooms for use during the night, and in the morning the contents were sometimes frozen solid. We could put enough blankets on the beds to stay warm during the night, but getting out of bed in the morning was, shall we say, stimulating.

For Christmas I had received a pair of ice skates, the kind you strap to the bottom of your shoes. They were hand-me-downs from my cousin Roger Booth, but they were no less precious to me for that. I had noticed that there was a frozen lagoon in a wheat field a couple of miles from our place, and I was eager to try out the skates. To get there I would have to cross Dead Man's Gulch, a miniature Grand Canyon a mile or two long and up to a hundred feet deep. We owned the deepest part of it. It had sheer clay walls, weird formations, and labyrinthine tributaries, some of which were clogged with cedar trees.

Mother thought it was too dangerous for me to go alone. I was eight, but I thought I was practically grown. I nagged and argued so persistently that finally she gave in. "All right, go! You're too big for your britches, so you go right ahead! Just stop pestering me and go!"

So I trudged off across the snow, found a place to cross the gulch, and got to the lagoon. The wind was viciously cold. I had to take my mittens off to adjust the skates, so my hands were freezing. The skates wouldn't stay on. The ice was rough from windblown snow that had melted and refrozen in waves on top of the ice. But having made such a fuss to get there, I was determined to skate. By the time I gave up, the sun was giving up too, disappearing into the frozen treeless horizon far across the dark gash of Dead Man's Gulch.

When I got back to the gulch, it was getting dark and I couldn't find the spot where I had crossed. The walls seemed too steep to go down, let alone climb back up. In desperation I finally fell and slid to the bottom, and then found that it was even darker down there. I walked a long way along the bottom until I found a place where I could climb out. By the time I got home it was completely dark. When I opened the door, Mother swept me into her arms, sobbing, and held me. "Oh, I should never have let you go! You could have drowned, or froze to death. I couldn't leave the others to come look for you. Thank God you're alive!"

That's the only time I can recall either of my parents second-guessing themselves about a decision to let me do something. Generally they trusted me to look out for myself and didn't waste time worrying about what would happen if I didn't. Even on that occasion, I don't think my father was worried. He probably reasoned that the lagoon was too shallow to drown in; that if I got lost I could find the north star and head west; and that if I couldn't climb out of the gulch I would have sense enough to walk downhill until I reached the mouth, where there was a road that would eventually bring me back toward home.

Several times I tried to find out how Dead Man's Gulch got its name. The neighbors shrugged and said, "That's just what people call it." Finally I heard the story, from an old man who didn't remember it very clearly. "It used to be called Devil's Gulch," he said. "A hot-headed young feller was courting a girl that lived where the Minnick place is now. One night when it was pitch-black he left there riding hell-bent for leather. The horse went right into the gulch and landed on top of the feller."

It was an unsatisfactory explanation. Why did he leave the place riding hard, especially on a pitch-black night? Didn't he know about the gulch? A horse can see very well at night and would surely have tried to avoid the gulch; did the rider deliberately spur the horse over the cliff? What had happened at the girl's house? I never found anyone who knew, or even showed much interest in the questions. Later I heard that there was a terrible lightning storm that night, but that only deepens the mystery. Did the girl or her parents turn the traveler out into such a storm? The horse and rider weren't electrocuted, so how did the storm cause their deaths? I guess the answers are lost in Dead Man's Gulch.

At Maywood we were to have the advantage of town school; I suspect that was an argument Dad used to get Mother to move there. All twelve grades were in one homely brick cube, two or three stories high. My grade, the fourth, shared a room and a teacher with the fifth and sixth grades. For many years I thought my memory of the teacher, Miss Herrick, must be a caricature, a distortion created by my fear and hatred of her. Then I saw a photo of her, and she was exactly as I remembered her. She was an older woman—old maid, we would have said then. Her graying hair was pulled back severely into a bun and she wore round wire rimmed glasses. Her face was pinched into a grimace in which her teeth were perpetually bared; perhaps it was only an expression of determination, but it looked to me like she had fangs.

Keeping order and administering discipline were her priorities. It's true that there were some rowdy fifth- and sixth-grade boys in the class, but whether that was the cause or effect of her methods is open to question. She must have done some teaching, but all I remember is Miss Herrick patrolling the aisles while we were all supposed to be studying. She carried a wooden stick about four feet long and as thick as her thumb. She liked to patrol from the back of the room to the front. When they heard her approaching behind them, kids cringed but dared not look up. We were sure she had eyes in the back of her head. If a boy smirked or mocked her after she walked by, she whirled and slammed the stick down on his shoulders. The stick was so long she could reach across to the second row of desks.

She used the stick first and spoke second; if she saw a wrong answer on someone's paper, or someone reading the wrong assignment, she slammed the stick on the desk and then explained what the offender was doing wrong. Older boys said she had been known to hit kids on the head or ears and make them bleed. I don't believe that now, but I believed it then. Miss Herrick never struck me or even my desk, but I was terrified of her.

A few weeks into the spring term, my sisters and I all came down with chicken pox. For the week or ten days that we couldn't go to school, we spent all day in the dining room where it was warm, huddled around the gas lamp reading or playing games. I don't remember feeling bad, but even if I had it would have been worth it to avoid school.

I got well just in time to humiliate myself at school on Valentine's Day. The prettiest girl in the room was a fourth-grader named Kathleen. She had blue eyes, golden finger curls, fair skin, and the reddest lips I had ever seen. I was smitten. For several days we brought valentines for our friends and put them in a decorated box at the front of the room, to be opened on Valentine's Day. I wanted to do something special for Kathleen, so I bought her a big chocolate heart and wrapped it in paper. When the time came to put it in the box I was already aflame with self-consciousness, and when I got to the front of the room, I discovered to my horror that my supervalentine was too big to go in the slot. Mortified and confused, I left it beside the box. Everyone was watching. They soon satisfied their curiosity as to the intended recipient, and they teased me unmercifully. Worse, they teased Kathleen too, which of course made her detest me.

Not long after that I discovered the art of malingering, inspired no doubt by the warm snug joy of staying home with chicken pox. After arriving at school I began to "not feel good." In my heart of hearts I knew I wasn't sick, but it was also true that I *didn't* feel good. I was sick with fear of Miss Herrick, longing for the friendly world at Union, and humiliation over the Valentine affair. Getting out of school was surprisingly easy. The superintendent couldn't very well tell me I wasn't sick if I said I was. He couldn't call my parents to come get me because our phone didn't work, and he couldn't drive me home himself, because he taught high school classes. So he recruited one of his high school students, Dick, to drive me home.

Dick was happy to get out of class, and once he learned the route he became my regular ambulance driver as well as my friend. He had a 1936 Chevy with a good heater and the reassuring smell of mohair upholstery. After a few minutes in Dick's car I always felt better—but not well enough to go back to school. Mother was dismayed to see me coming home, but she never sent me back. I suspect she understood that the childhood diseases include more than physical ailments.

I went home sick one or two days a week for most of the term. I understood that I had to go to school most of the time, but the days that I stayed were still miserable. I had a couple of friends but I was still the new kid, often alone. I began to walk to Main Street during lunch hour, to buy a piece of candy or bubble gum at Perkin Mercantile Company. Perkin's was the town's general store—clothing and hardware on one side, groceries on the other—run by Ina and Grace Perkin, both in their 80's.

I later learned that the Perkin sisters were victims of a bizarre family agreement. Their father, Joe Perkin, had founded the store and made it successful. When he died he left it to his children, three daughters and a son, subject to an agreement that any of them who married would forfeit his or her share. One sister did so, and the son died, leaving Ina and Grace locked in spinsterly ownership.

I began to loiter at Perkin's, reading comic books or coveting the merchandise. Ina and Grace were old and inattentive, and I began stealing cigarettes, mostly Old Golds. I took them home and smoked them in the outhouse, sometimes smoking an entire pack in an hour or two. One day I picked up a candy bar and headed for the door. One of the sisters—I couldn't tell them apart—intercepted me and said, "What do you have in your hand?" I was backed up against a counter and I pressed the candy bar up under the lip of the counter with one hand. I extended the empty hand for Miss Perkin's inspection.

"No, the other hand," she said. I was caught chocolate-handed, and visions of reform school or at least public humiliation flashed through my mind. Instead, I got a private humiliation. She said, "Son, if you're hungry and you don't have any money, you tell me and I'll give you something. That's nothing to be ashamed of. But stealing is." The words shriveled me.

*Fourth, fifth, and sixth grades at
Maywood, 1947–1948. Miss Herrick
is third from left, back row. In the
middle of the back row (with dark
hair) is Donna Gilliland, the rodeo
queen I hoped to impress at the
Curtis rodeo. That's me on the left
in the front row; the blonde at fifth
from left in the same row is Kathleen,
my Valentine sweetheart.*

[8]

The Great Cattle Drive

MY MAYWOOD MEMORIES AREN'T ALL BAD. Among the best are those of the great cattle drive. Our cattle had wintered at Maywood, but they were to summer in our old pastures just off the valley. In the fall Dad had hired two or three tractor-trailers to haul them to Maywood, but in the spring he decided to trail them back instead of trucking them. He explained that it would save money, but I think he was also taken by the romance of a latter-day trail drive.

For an eight-year-old, it was a cowboy dream come true. It would be a two-day, forty-mile trip, camping out overnight, and I would get to go. It wasn't exactly the cowboy life that Andy Adams described, but I knew it was as close as I would ever get.

On the morning we were to leave, around May 1, the cattle were gathered in a small pasture. Dad and the other horsemen—my cousin Roger Booth and a couple of neighbors—were mounted up, and we were about to set out when a car appeared on the track leading from town. As it got closer, I saw to my horror that it was the school superintendent. It was a school day and I was playing hooky again, this time without even pretending to be sick. I was devastated, certain that I would be snatched from the experience of a lifetime and deposited back in Miss Herrick's hated classroom.

Dad and the superintendent talked for a while out of my hearing, looking my way occasionally. Finally the superintendent left and Dad came over to me. A defendant standing before a judge for sentencing in a capital case could not have been more apprehensive than I was at that moment.

Dad said, "I told him we need you. I told him you won't miss any more days after this, and you won't."

It is remarkable that a human heart can stand such a violent emotional turnabout, from deepest despair to inexpressible exhilaration in an instant. I'm surprised mine didn't burst.

I didn't get to ride because I didn't have a horse, and that was a big disappointment. But I did have a working role. We trailed the cattle, forty or fifty cows plus their calves, along dirt roads east across the table to an intersection north of Moorefield, which was almost a ghost town. From there we went north up Moorefield canyon, across the divide that separates the Platte and Republican watersheds, and down some more canyons to the Platte Valley. Mother drove the car ahead of the herd to flag down any oncoming drivers who might not see the herd just over a hill or around a curve. My job was to ride with Mother and jump out and close any open gates that might let the cattle stray from the right-of-way into a field or pasture. At intersections I got out and guarded the wrong road long enough to get the lead cows started down the right road, stayed until one of the riders from the rear came up to keep the rest of the herd from taking the wrong road, then ran ahead to the car.

On the first day things went well until we came to Fox Creek. A flood had washed out the bridge there and the county had laid some planks across the narrow stream. The temporary bridge was just inches above the water and barely wide enough for one car. Mother and I held our breath while we drove across it. The planks bounced and rumbled, but we made it. But the cattle wouldn't cross it. The riders yelled and waved hats and ropes, pressing the herd toward the creek, trying to force one or two onto the planks. They would put their noses to the end of the planks, but their eyes rolled with fear and they wouldn't step onto the wood.

Finally Dad signaled the men to back off and let the cattle settle down. After a few minutes Dad dismounted and walked among the cows until he found the one he wanted—a sensible old cow that he knew would do his bidding. He gently herded her onto the planks, and once she was across, the others followed willingly.

We camped that night at an abandoned farmstead in the canyon north of Moorefield. We put the cattle in the old corrals and the horses in the empty barn. We had planned to cook over a campfire and sleep outside, but a light rain began to fall, so we moved into the house. The house had been vacant for many years; some of the windows were broken, and the house smelled of dust and decay. In the main room was a huge pack rat pile. Pack rats make their nests from found objects, and they especially like anything that shines. In the pile of twigs, rags, and leaves were many pieces of tinfoil, tin can lids, and pieces of broken glass.

Mother cooked supper over a portable camp stove and then went home for the night. When the men realized I was staying the night with them, they began discussing pack rats:

"They're big devils, way bigger'n ordinary rats."

"They can carry more than their own weight. They gang up and two or three of 'em work together to move something really big."

"I've heard if a dog has on a bright metal tag, they'll sneak up on him while he's asleep and drag him off."

"Son, no more'n you weigh, you better take off that belt before you go to bed. One of 'em'll see that shiny buckle and carry you right off with it."

I knew they were just trying to scare me. Still, it was obvious pack rats did like to pick up things and carry them off, including people things. We spread our bedrolls on the floor in another room, but there was no door between us and the pack rat nest. I told myself that pack rats wouldn't come around people, but I wasn't positive of that. My ears strained for sounds of rats. It was cold and damp, and every time I started to doze off some unfamiliar noise would jolt me awake. I hardly slept at all. Judging by the tossing and turning I heard during the night, and the bleary eyes I saw at breakfast the next morning, nobody else slept well either. It made me think maybe they weren't just teasing me after all. Maybe they believed those stories about pack rats themselves. But for me certainly, and probably for them, one sleepless night was a small price to pay for a chance to be part of an honest-to-God cattle drive in the middle of the twentieth century.

The people we saw along the way may have thought we were

crazy. Although farmers occasionally drove cattle across the road from one pasture to another, and maybe along the road for a mile or two, by that time nobody drove them forty miles. But most of the people we encountered smiled and waved; our anachronistic project must have given them some pleasure too.

Our only unfriendly encounter came early on the second day. We were approaching a ramshackle farmstead when a heifer took a notion to leave the road and head for the hills. The nearest rider was my cousin Roger. He was only thirteen, but he was the best cowboy in the group. He rode his own buckskin horse called—what else—Buck. Roger nudged the horse and Buck tore across what appeared to be a small plowed field to head off the heifer. A man ran out of the house waving his arms and shaking his fists. He had on pants, but only his longjohns from the waist up.

"Goddammit, you ruined my garden! What's the matter with you crazy bastards! Get that Goddamned horse out of my garden! You'll pay for this, Goddammit!"

Roger was already two-thirds of the way across the plot, and I'm not sure he could hear exactly what the man was saying. In any event, there wasn't any other way to retrieve the heifer, so he continued on and brought her back.

Later somebody asked Roger what he would have done if the man had come out of the house with a gun.

"I'd have let him have the heifer," Roger said.

Back at school, where all the boys wanted to be cowboys, telling about the cattle drive made me the envy of all. One of them, a bully named Keith, tried to make something of the fact that I wasn't on horseback, but I didn't let it get under my skin. I had been there, and he hadn't.

[9]

Rodeo Man

ONCE SCHOOL WAS OUT, life at Maywood wasn't so bad. Summer brought more adventures. Mother found a rattlesnake in the yard and killed it with a garden hoe. Dad bought hundreds of little trees by mail order to make a windbreak north of the buildings. When they came they looked like dead twigs. Nevertheless, we all pitched in to plant them—Russian olives to grow quickly, ash to provide more permanent shade, and firs to break the wind. The only means of watering them was with five-gallon buckets carried from the windmill fifty yards away. Over the summer Mother and Dad carried hundreds of buckets of water to keep the seedlings alive. They survived, and remnants of the windbreak can still be seen from far across the hills.

On one corner of our land was a prairie dog town. Their watchfulness was fascinating. They stood at attention at the mouth of their holes, chattering to each other about the human intruder, and seemed willing to do that forever, or at least longer than I was willing to stay. But ranchers of our day detested prairie dogs the way those of an earlier day detested sodbusters. It was universally assumed that cattle and horses broke their legs in prairie dog holes, though current scientific wisdom says that isn't so.

Whatever the scientists say, it *is* true that rattlesnakes like to hibernate in prairie dog holes; we sometimes saw them warming themselves just outside the holes on sunny days in early spring. And there is no denying that prairie dogs dig up a lot of grass. To our minds, any of these was sufficient reason to exterminate them. We did it by asphyxiating them with carbon monoxide. We attached one end of a hose to the exhaust pipe of a truck and stuffed the other end in the prairie dog den.

Cute as they were, I don't recall having any sense of regret about seeing them gassed; I guess I was already acculturated at age eight.

Not far from the prairie dog town was a pasture full of the wildest cattle I have ever seen. They belonged to a neighbor who was said to be as wild as his cattle, though I don't recall seeing him. His cattle were like wild animals—wide-eyed, fleet, and reclusive.

The most notable among them was a huge stag. That's what we called a steer who had escaped half way through the process of being castrated and got away with one testicle intact, thereby becoming half bull and half steer, with the worst traits of both.

The neighbor's stag had never been caught again. He appeared to be four or five years old and was tall as a horse. His horns were not wide like a longhorn's, but curved upwards a foot or more and ended in sharp points. He carried his head high like a deer.

People said the neighbor was afraid to try to corral the stag, and I didn't blame him. Dad devoted extra care to maintaining our fence lest he would have to venture into the neighbor's pasture to retrieve a stray.

We had a yearling colt, Cedar, half saddle horse and half work horse. He got a bad barbed wire cut on his chest. Dad said not to worry about it, it would heal on its own, but it looked awful. My sister Nancy and I both thought it needed medical attention.

The best horseman in the area was our nearest neighbor, Harry Corlett, who lived a couple of miles away on Medicine Creek. We were forbidden to go that far by ourselves, but Nancy and I decided to take Cedar for a consultation with Harry. Cedar was too young to be ridden, so we led him cross-country, through the cattle underpass under Highway 83 and through several barbed-wire gates, stopping along the way to watch tumblebugs make perfect balls of manure. We saw a snake but didn't kill it because it was just a bull snake.

Harry painted Cedar's wound with Absorbine Jr. and put a little in a jar for us to take home and apply until the wound healed, and assured us Cedar would be fine. When we got home we confessed what we had done and got a serious scolding, which we considered a small price to pay for (as we thought) saving Cedar's life.

Our other illicit activity was calf riding. There was a pen of young calves behind the barn, out of sight of the house. Dad didn't want us riding them because he wanted them to gain weight as fast as possible, not lose it trying to buck us off. Nancy was as big as I, though two years younger, and probably tougher. One of us would grab a calf by the head and pin it against the fence while the other got on. We didn't have a rope so we tied baling wire around the calf's belly. We learned that if you took six or eight strands and twisted them together the wire wouldn't cut your hands when the calf bucked. We both became pretty good calf riders.

One day in late June, in the window of Perkin's store, I saw a poster for the Fourth of July rodeo at Curtis, the next town east. What caught my eye was the list of rodeo events, which included kids' steer riding. I asked Dad if I could enter.

"You're too little," he said.

I kept arguing my case. "I'm nine, Dad. It doesn't say you have to be any certain age."

"Yeah, but you're little for your age. How big are those steers? You don't even know."

Dad wouldn't yield, but he did agree to let me go to the rodeo with Harry Anderson. Harry was no kin, but he was working for us as a hired hand. He was a jolly, pink-faced man, totally bald, with jug ears. He was notoriously windy; he had a high sing-song voice which he rarely let rest. My parents and sisters were going to a family Fourth of July gathering in the valley, so they dropped Harry and me off at Curtis and were to pick us up again that night.

We arrived in Curtis before mid-morning and Harry headed straight for a beer joint. It was Sunday morning, but the bar was already full of holiday celebrants. The place smelled terrible and there was nothing for me to do. Harry soon forgot about me, so I walked to the rodeo grounds at the edge of town. When I got there I found the rodeo secretary and asked if she was still taking entries for the steer riding. She said yes, so I entered. I think all I had to do was give her my name.

I went to the watermelon stand and bought a big slice for lunch. There I ran into my friend from the valley, Joe Tetro. His father, Ken, was entered in the calf roping. Joe wasn't entered in the steer riding because he was hurt. He was eleven or twelve and his father had been teaching him to rope calves. He had just graduated from roping a dummy calf off a stationary horse to the real thing. Unlike a wooden horse, a roping horse stops violently. The saddle horn had smashed Joe in the groin. We went behind a tree and he unbuttoned his jeans and showed me the damage: one testicle was the size and color of an eggplant.

I also saw Donna Gilliland, who was as close to an idol in my eyes as any female was likely to get. I knew her from school at Maywood. She was five years older than I, already a rodeo queen, an accomplished horsewoman, and a member of a rodeo family. Most importantly, she had beautiful curves and she was always sweet to me. Being able to tell her I was entered in the steer riding inflated me with nine-year-old machismo.

The steer riding was the first event. I went to the steer-riding chute as soon as I saw activity there, and told the man in charge my name.

"You ridin'?" he said. "You're too little. Your folks here?"

I told him no, but I was nine years old, and they had given me permission.

"You sure about that? I think we better ask Eddie."

Harry Corlett's brother, Eddie, was the head of the Curtis Roping Club and was in charge of the rodeo. He was also the announcer, so he was in the booth above the main bucking chutes. The man from the steer-riding chute led me across the arena and we stood in front of the bucking chutes and talked up to Eddie.

"This little kid here wants to ride a steer but his folks ain't here. He says it's okay with them, but we got no way to know."

Harry Corlett was in the arena, mounted on his pickup horse. He recognized me and rode over. Eddie explained the issue to Harry.

"Your dad say it was all right?" Harry asked me.

"Sure did," I lied. "Just this morning. He had Harry Anderson come over here with me so I could do it."

"Where's he?"

"I don't know. I left him in the beer joint this morning."

Harry looked at me a long time. I felt like a dwarf, looking up at Harry on horseback and Eddie in the announcer's box, and I knew I must look puny to them. Harry knew my dad well enough to know that he wouldn't be likely to let me ride, especially when he wasn't present. But Harry was a rodeo man and would have been happy to let me ride if I had been his son. Finally he turned to Eddie. "Well, he says it's all right with his dad, so I don't see why he can't."

The man at the steer-riding chute picked out the smallest steer for me. It was still twice as big as the calves I had ridden at home, and it had nubbins—the beginnings of horns, an inch or so long. The man put my steer in the chute first, so I was the very first rider of the rodeo. Eddie, the announcer, made a big to-do over the loudspeaker about me being the littlest contestant. I rode the steer a few jumps and then got bucked off. The arena dirt was soft and deep, and as I ran back toward the chute the dirt pulled off one of my boots. They were hand-me-downs from Roger Booth, a size or two too big. I retrieved the boot and ran out of the arena with one on and one off, and the crowd laughed. It didn't matter, I was proud and deliriously happy.

The steer riding wasn't a competitive event: they gave each kid who entered a silver dollar. I had never had one before and was amazed at how heavy it was. With it in my pocket, I felt like I walked lopsided.

After the rodeo I walked back to town and tried to find Harry Anderson, but the bars were too crowded for a person as short as me to find anyone. I went to the city park, where a variety show was performing in a tent. They were a latter-day vaudeville troupe, merchants and schoolteachers who could sing or dance or act. They traveled around our part of Nebraska bringing people the only live theater most of them would ever see. I sneaked into the tent and saw a Lincoln County celebrity, Charlie Craig, who drew caricatures and told jokes, and a beautiful woman who sang and tap-danced.

It had been a glorious day of adventure, independence, and triumph. When my parents picked me up, I couldn't resist showing them my silver dollar and telling them how I had earned it. I told them the story I had rehearsed in my mind all afternoon: I ran into Harry Corlett at the rodeo and he talked me into riding the steer. I didn't want to do it and told him that Dad wouldn't let me, but Harry insisted.

I didn't see the transparency of my lie because my parents acted as if they believed it. They let me revel in my pride, and never let on that they doubted my story. I paid a price, however. Harry and his wife Melva sometimes came over for Sunday dinner, and every time I heard they were coming I was stricken with fear that my parents would say something about Harry talking me into riding the steer, or Harry would reveal that I had claimed to have permission. Instead, they would bring up the subject of the steer riding and look at each other with sly smiles while I squirmed.

If Harry Corlett was my guilty conscience, Harry Anderson was my Boswell. If he was at the dinner table with us when the subject came up, he would launch into his own windy account of the event:

"Here come Davy out of the chute, that ole steer blowin' smoke out of his nose"—Harry snorted and lowered his head like a bull—"Davy hangin' on for dear life. The steer ducked to the left"—Harry dropped his left shoulder—"then he ducked to the right"—another gesture to the other side—"and ole Davy was stayin' right in the middle. Then that ole steer jumped about six feet high, and ole Davy's boot come off and flew twenty foot in the air"—Harry waved his arms and kicked one foot high in the air—"When that steer come down, Davy went one way and the boot went the other."

Everybody laughed, but I knew they were laughing at Harry, not me. I doubt that Harry ever made it to the rodeo that day, and if he did he would have been in no condition to recognize me. He had put the story together in his mind, from snippets he had heard, and it was as real to him as if he had seen it. In a world less wedded to unvarnished truth, Harry's love of storytelling would have been appreciated. In our world, Harry was just a blowhard.

Before the summer was over, my parents decided to move back to the valley. I'm sure part of the reason was the discovery that town school wasn't necessarily superior to Union School. More importantly, we all missed the Union community. Maywood was a nice little town and my parents made some lifelong friends during the nine months we lived there, but we didn't belong the way we did at Union.

We hadn't given up the lease on our old place on the valley, and the hired man who was farming it for us hadn't worked out. By the time school started we had moved back into the house and the Union community as if we had never been gone.

For several years after we moved back to the valley we still owned the Maywood place. I often went there with Dad to work cattle, fix fence, or harvest hay in the wet bottoms of Medicine Creek. We bounced over the forty miles of gravel road in an old pickup, a long dust plume following us. The long drowsy trip was fun. Dad sometimes sang "Mexicali Rose" or "Springtime in the Rockies."

Sometimes I had to drive a tractor to or from the Maywood place, and that was not fun. There aren't many things more boring than sitting for four hours on a tractor going ten miles an hour through sparsely populated country with nothing to look at but an occasional windmill. I was grateful that there were few cars on the road, because when one passed me it threw dust and gravel up in my face.

There wasn't a hotel in Maywood, so when we stayed several days, we took a room above Verbeck's Café. A stair on the outside of the building led to two or three sleeping rooms with a shared toilet. For washing there was a big bowl and a water pitcher on a washstand in each room.

Mr. Verbeck seemed foreign, or maybe he was just an Easterner. He served smelly foods—things like cabbage and garlic and broccoli, I suppose—and the odors were powerful in the rooms above the café. Dad said we had to eat in the café once in a while so as not to insult Verbeck, but I thought the food tasted as bad as it smelled, and Dad wasn't fond of it either. We both preferred the little café a couple of blocks down the street, which served things like roast beef and mashed potatoes.

We were in Perkin Mercantile one day when an ancient little man dressed all in black came in. He was sunburned and unshaven and his clothes were shabby. He asked one of the Perkin sisters, "Do you have any scissors that need sharpened?" She asked how much he charged, and his answer was something minimal, maybe twenty cents.

She reached under the counter and brought out a couple of pairs of scissors, which I assume he sharpened after Dad and I left.

The next day as we drove back toward the valley we saw the little man squatting in the road ditch a few miles from Maywood. He had built a small fire and appeared to be cooking something. I asked Dad if he was a hobo, and Dad said, "No, that's just how he makes his living. It's a damn shame he isn't over on the valley. Over here he'll walk ten miles to find two customers. On the valley he'd have ten times as many."

My uncle, Ernie Booth, foreman of
the Upper 96 Ranch, circa 1945.

[10]

Horselessness

THE HAPPIEST TIMES OF MY BOYHOOD involved horses. My uncle, Earnest Booth, was foreman of the Upper 96 Ranch, ten miles up the valley from us. The Upper 96 had been a station for the Pony Express (as had the Lower 96, twenty miles farther down the valley). The 96 was a vast cattle operation so it had lots of horses, and Ernie was always willing to let me ride one.

Ernie had married my father's sister, Lucille. They were among my parents' closest friends, so we went there often for Sunday dinner. My cousin Roger was a few years older than I, and just as horse-crazy. After dinner, while Dad and Ernie hunted pheasants or pitched horse-shoes, Roger and I rode horses.

The ranch buildings were on the south bank of the Platte. Just across a shallow channel of the river lay Brady Island, ten miles long and two or three miles wide, named for a fur trapper who was murdered there in the 1830s. The Upper 96 owned much of the island and ran cattle there, and that's where Roger and I usually rode. The island was a mysterious wonderland, lightly wooded with cottonwoods, willows, and cedar. Except for the occasional barbed wire fence, there was no evidence of human habitation. We forded streams and dodged quicksand. Occasionally we would come upon a rotting carcass of a cow or a skeleton of some creature not clearly identifiable. It was easy to imagine Indians lurking behind a fat cedar tree or lying in ambush in one of the sandy channels that dried up when a beaver dam or a flood changed the stream's course.

Roger and I raced our horses, played horseback tag among the trees, and fought imaginary Indians. He rode his buckskin gelding, the best horse on the ranch, and I rode some aging horse deemed to be dull enough to pose no danger to a small boy. Roger seemed to me to be the best cowboy in the world, and in fact he later became a talented bull rider on the professional rodeo circuit. I couldn't hope to equal Roger in horsemanship, but he was generous with me, taught me most of what I know about horses, and didn't make fun of my sorry horse or ill-fitting saddle.

Ernie was a different matter. He made fun of everybody, especially anyone who was poorly mounted, badly outfitted, or lacking in horsemanship, and I was all three. Even so, he was my favorite uncle, and not only because he had horses.

Ernie was a charming bad boy. He had a gold tooth and a smile that was close to a leer. His complexion was perpetually red from sun and wind. He had a long torso with short legs and he walked with a swagger. He wore a sweat-stained, beat-up, small-brimmed 1930s-style cowboy hat. He rarely wore anything but a blue chambray work shirt, blue jeans, and worn-out boots. I never understood how his jeans stayed up. He had no hips. He wasn't a fat man but he had a big belly, and his belt hovered in its shadow, somewhere just above indecent exposure.

He was one of five boys whose father died when the eldest was eleven. When her husband's death left her destitute, the mother, Marie, put her five boys in a horse-drawn wagon and homesteaded in the sandhills of northwest Custer County where there was still unclaimed land in the early 20th century. The boys got little schooling. They helped their mother work the homestead and later worked on a large ranch in the area. They acquired a reputation throughout Custer County as the rough and ready Booth boys. Marie was a tough, gravel-voiced woman much beloved in her old age by the large clan of descendants that her boys produced.

Ernie was loud and profane. He was rough with horses, cattle, and his children. His wife, Aunt Lucille, was exactly the opposite. She was sweet, shy, gentle, and unfailingly pleasant. Different as they were, the chemistry between Ernie and her was powerful. He would leer at her and touch her breast or pat her bottom. She would blush and say, "Ernie, cut it out!" but her smile said, "I like that." They were the only couple I knew that I can imagine slipping off to bed in the afternoon.

Sometimes I stayed a day or two with the Booths. If the weather was good, Roger and I would ride all day. If it was cold or wet, we would hang out with the ranch hands—in the bunkhouse if it was Sunday or, if it was any other day, in the barn where the men were put to work oiling and repairing tack or cleaning out stalls. Visiting the 96 was as close as I ever got to living the life of a ranch hand, and I loved it.

But unless I was visiting the Booths, I could never be sure of having a horse. My father, like many of our neighbors, was deeply conflicted about the legitimacy of cowboying in our lives. On the one hand, the cowboy tradition was part of our birthright. Most all of us raised cattle, our land had originally been settled by cattlemen, and there were still several great ranches in the vicinity. But it was becoming obvious that the cowboy was no longer essential to the cattle business, or even very useful. When pastures contained a section of land or more, you needed a horse to round up the cattle. Now many ranchers realize that pastures that big are inefficient. Cattle are lazy and they try not to venture very far from water. They overgraze the portion of the pasture nearest the windmill and ignore the plentiful grass in the far reaches of the pasture. So if the rancher wants to make money and take care of his land, he subdivides his pastures and moves the cattle frequently from one small pasture to another.

You don't need a horse to gather the cattle from a pasture of two or three hundred acres. You just wait until the heat of the day when they're all around the water tank, drive in among them in your pickup and offer them a little cottonseed cake, and they'll follow you to the new pasture. Chasing them on horseback just makes them wild and causes them to run off pounds that you don't want them to lose.

My father and most of our neighbors were practical, unsentimental men. But they were also tugged by the romance of the disappearing cowboy life. Most of them had seen the real cowboy era, at least in their boyhood. In the 1930s my father had been a ranch hand in Montana, and he loved to tell of trailing cattle or sheep to mountain pastures in summer, sleeping under the stars, living on bacon and beans for weeks at a time. In these men, the lure of the disappearing cowboy life was at war with the sober ethic of doing things the modern, efficient way. As is often true of conflicted people, their occasional surrenders to romance were sometimes followed by angry repudiations of that impulse.

For the first nine years of my life, the anti-cowboy impulse won out in our household. We often had a horse on loan from a neighbor, but we didn't have one of our own. My father put me on borrowed ponies and horses from the time I was a toddler, and I learned to ride as naturally as a baby learns to walk. My parents were usually willing to let me ride as I grew older, but I was always at someone else's mercy. I had to take whatever was offered—usually the sorriest horse and a saddle with stirrups I couldn't reach. Worst of all was the uncertainty, the fear that I might be left out of the adventure of the moment for want of a horse.

So I spent my early years lurching between the ecstasy of being a horseman and the emotional desolation of being afoot. I had school-mates who cared nothing about horses, but for me they were the most important thing in the world. All I wanted to be was a cowboy, and when that's your aspiration, being horseless guarantees that you will be disappointed, excluded, and humiliated. In the cowboy world, if you have a horse—a decent horse, one people won't laugh at—you are a free man, heir to the great traditions and myths of the West. But until I was ten, I could never be sure whether my cowboy dreams would be fulfilled or dashed.

*Me, riding a borrowed pony at
the 96 Ranch, circa 1950.*

[11]

Working Cattle

THE PAIN OF NOT HAVING A HORSE was worst at branding time, always the third week in June. That was the very best week of the year. Tuesday, Wednesday, and Thursday were branding days and Friday, Saturday, and Sunday of that week were always the dates of the Buffalo Bill Rodeo in North Platte.

Branding was the major roundup of the year. It was the one occasion of the year when everyone surrendered to the cowboy tradition and worked horseback. We, the Clarks, and the Tetros collaborated. The crew included my father and me; Jim Clark and his three sons, Roger, Dale, and Van; and Ken Tetro, his son Joe, and his hired man, John Workman. On Tuesday we worked our herd of less than a hundred cows. Wednesday we worked Jim Clark's slightly larger herd. On Thursday we worked the Tetros' herd of two hundred cows or more.

Until I got my own horse, I didn't get to ride unless the Tetros had an extra horse. Sometimes they did, sometimes not. The best I could hope for was Buster, a kid horse who was slow and lazy. There was no saddle small enough for me so I rode an adult saddle with my feet tucked into the straps above the stirrups.

The days leading up to branding were agonizing, as I waited to find out if Buster would be available for me. One year I didn't get to ride because Ken's daughter Terre, about my age, decided she wanted to go. The humiliation of being afoot when a girl was mounted was crushing. Another year I didn't get to ride because one of Ken's town friends decided he wanted to ride. My disappointment was no less, but I got some pleasure from the sight of a grown man ignominiously mounted on a horse spiritless enough for a seven-year-old boy.

When I did get to ride, it was even better than riding with Roger at the 96, because the roundups were real cowboy work. We saddled our horses before dawn and rode off toward the pastures at first light. There was always a chilly dampness in the air, and sometimes it was drizzling. Sometimes one of the horses, feeling frisky in the cold morning air, would buck a little. For some reason, Dale Clark usually got the horse most likely to buck. He didn't have his own mount and wasn't considered horseman enough to get one of the savvy cowhorses that Ken and Dad rode. But he was a young man, lanky and strong, and therefore presumed to be able to handle anything. And, as someone was always sure to observe, if he got killed there would be no widow or orphans, because Dale was a bachelor. If the horse bucked, we all cheered and hooted at Dale for grabbing the saddle horn.

The pastures were a few miles back in the clay hills and canyons south of the valley. Each was at least two hundred acres. Ken Tetro was a holdout for the old ways of ranching, so most of the Tetro pastures were a full section, 640 acres. We split off one or two at a time to work different pastures. They were rugged but almost treeless, and flushing out the cattle was surprisingly easy.

We rode the tops of the ridges so we could see down the slope on either side and into the pockets and canyons at the bottom. When we saw cattle we trotted or galloped toward them shouting and waving an arm or a hat. That started them running like water down the hillsides toward the canyons and down the canyons toward bigger canyons. If you saw a pocket with a stand of trees, you had to ride down and make sure no cattle were hiding there. Experienced hands knew where the cattle were likely to be, taking into account the weather, the condition of the grass and water, and the habits of cows. Ken or Dad could cover a bigger pasture than the rest of us because it took them less time to find all the cattle.

Cattle would rather travel down a flat canyon bottom than climb the hills, so ranchers locate the gates between pastures in the canyon bottoms. Once we got the cattle into a canyon, we pushed them through the opening in the fence and met up with the cattle and riders from the next pasture. Eventually the different streams of cattle came together in a major canyon and the riders all joined up to herd them down that canyon to the corrals.

At that point the roundup became a cattle drive. The best hands—usually Ken and Dad or Jim Clark—rode point. They galloped along the sides of the canyon, sometimes part way up the adjoining ridges, keeping the leaders of the herd from breaking out of the canyon. The next best riders worked the sides of the herd farther back, turning back any independent thinkers who might not be inclined to follow the leaders. The rest of us were pushers, riding drag. We brought up the rear, trying to keep the herd moving at a brisk pace, thwarting cutbacks, shouting and slapping stragglers and sometimes nudging them with the chests of our horses. If the weather was dry we breathed dust and flies. If it was wet we were splattered with mud and manure.

In hot weather the cattle tired quickly and it was hard to keep them moving. If it was cold they were wild and would try to turn back or break out. As we got close to the corrals the cattle seemed to realize what was ahead and they would almost always make a move. The point men knew when and where it was likely to come, but it still pushed them and their mounts to the limit. A few cows somewhere behind the leaders would suddenly break out at full speed up a side pocket or a small ridge. The man riding point on that side would try to head them off, his horse jumping small ravines, plunging up hillsides, and sliding down steep slopes.

Usually the action was momentary. The renegades would be turned back quickly and the herd kept on course. But occasionally a point man got a late start or a horse stumbled and the breakout succeeded. When that happened, we saw what a fragile thing order is. In an instant, the smooth flow of the drive was destroyed. One group of riders had to go retrieve the runaways. A quick decision had to be made: should we keep pushing the main herd toward the corrals or wait up for the return of the breakaways? Ken was the unchallenged authority in such matters, and in a second or two he would signal whether we were to push on or wait up.

Most times we kept them moving, because it is easier to hold a herd together moving than standing. Unless the breakaways were returned shortly, however, we faced chaos at the corrals. It took a lot of shouting and waving to make the final push into the corrals. We had to make ourselves seem more threatening to the cattle than the smells and memories of the fences, chutes, and gates. If the riders bringing up the runaways caught up with us during those few moments of pandemonium, the sight and sound of it was likely to send the runaways off on another escape.

If there were no major breakaways, the cattle usually were in the corrals by nine o'clock. If I had suffered the indignity of being afoot, I was at the corrals waiting, having hitched a ride on the tractor that brought the trailer-mounted fly-sprayer up the canyon.

Once we had the cattle in the corrals, we became an efficient cattle-working machine. Calves were separated out into a series of pens that funneled through a narrow runway to the chute. The kids' job was to get in the pens with the calves, single one out, push it into the runway, and hold it there until the men working the chute were ready for it.

The trick of working the calf pens is to move up on the calf so fast it can't kick you. When you're pressed against the calf's rump it can beat its hind legs against your shins and step on your feet, but it can't really hurt you because it can't fully extend its leg. You learn the move pretty quickly because if you're too slow you get a hoof in the groin. When that happens, you reach for the nearest fence, slide between the poles, and fall on the grass outside the corral for a few minutes until you're able to get back in the pen.

The chute was a sort of trap, homemade of wood. Both ends were open, so when the gate at the end of the runway was opened the calf saw daylight through the chute and tried to break for freedom. The chute man had to squeeze the chute shut on the calf at just the right instant—too soon and the calf would duck back, too late and it would escape. The chute captured the calf just behind the head, and the chute man then tipped the chute—and calf—onto its side on the ground. The heeler, seated on the ground, grabbed one of the kicking hind legs in his hands and pulled it back, pushing the other hind leg forward with his foot. The calf was immobilized but exposed, so all operations could be done simultaneously. One man would brand the calf on the hip or ribs, another would clip an identifying tag or notch in the ear, another would inject vaccines for various bovine diseases, and another would castrate the bull calves.

Branding and castration were the jobs that required the most skill. The branding iron had to be just the right temperature—too cool and it wouldn't leave a permanent mark, too hot and it would make too deep a wound. For the same reasons, it had to be held against the hide just the right length of time, and rocked slightly from side to side to account for the slight curvature of the calf's side. If the weather was damp, you also had to account for the calf's wet hair, which would cool the iron a bit before it touched the hide.

In the earliest years that I remember, the irons were heated by red-hot coals from a wood fire, but it was hard to keep the fire just right, so in later years we used a gas-fired flame-thrower adapted to hold the branding irons at the right spot in the flame. With either source of heat you needed several irons so the one you had just used could be reheating while you branded the next calf. Jim Clark was the acknowledged expert with the branding iron.

Ken Tetro or Dad usually did the castrating, and both were skillful surgeons. They used a type of pocket knife called a stockman's knife, which has one blade shaped like a scalpel. If you keep the blade honed razor-sharp and know what you're doing, it takes only a few seconds to make a bull calf a steer. The testicles were tossed into a tall coffee can, to be served later as Rocky Mountain oysters.

It was hard, hot (or sometimes wet), messy, dangerous work. Hot irons, sharp knives, and long needles did their business inches away from hands holding struggling animals. Kids got kicked and men got nicks and scratches, but I don't remember anyone ever getting seriously hurt.

The goal was to average a calf a minute, and sometimes we did better. We were done by early afternoon, even with the Tetros' big herd. Since that was the last day—or maybe just because Ken liked to do it—we celebrated when we finished with his cattle. Before we left the corrals he brought out a washtub full of ice and Pabst Blue Ribbon beer. Then we caravanned down the canyon a few miles to the Tetros' place. He always invited his city friends to watch the branding, and if they decided they wanted to ride back to the valley, I was usually one of those who had to surrender his horse to the town folks.

Sometimes we made detours. Once Dale Clark found a strange plum tree during the roundup and led us back to it after the branding was done. It was covered with a species of big yellow plums none of us had seen before, and I haven't seen since. The sweet tangy plums tasted heavenly in our dusty throats. We picked as many as we could carry in our hats and ate them as we rode down the canyon to the valley.

Another time Dale scared up a coyote during the early morning roundup. He chased it into its burrow and plugged the opening with his shirt. After the branding he led us back to the burrow. Removing the shirt and shining a light into the hole, we discovered that it was a mother with pups. Somebody found a length of barbed wire, and by shoving one end into the hole and twisting the wire until it snagged in the coyotes' fur, we dragged them out to the mouth of the hole, one by one, and killed them.

The county was paying a bounty on coyotes at that time, a dollar and a half per head, so one of the men scalped the coyotes. The scalps were given either to Joe or to me—we're both equally sure that he's the one who collected the money.

Our view of coyotes was about like our view of prairie dogs: the only good one is a dead one. We believed coyotes killed calves, and that was like stealing money from a rancher's wallet. In fact, it was worse, because finding a newborn calf gutted by coyotes also sickened the heart. I now believe most of those calves were already dead by the time the coyotes arrived, but that possibility didn't occur to us then. Each coyote probably caught a hundred rabbits and a thousand gophers, varmints that would have eaten or dug up more grass than a calf was worth. But that benefit was invisible, while the dead calf was palpable and visceral. Irrational as it was, the hatred of coyotes was so universal that even at age eight or ten, I could watch the execution of cute coyote pups without a tremor of regret.

Back at the Tetros' house, we cleaned the blood and manure off our clothes as best we could and played blackjack on a blanket on the lawn while Dorothy fried up the Rocky Mountain oysters. One time the men let me win a hand or two, so I went home with a pocket full of nickels. I couldn't resist bragging about my winnings, which led to a scolding from Mother for both Dad and me.

We usually didn't get to go to the rodeo in North Platte unless it was rainy—if the weather was good we had to catch up on field work that had accumulated while we were busy with branding. The times we did get to go, the Buffalo Bill Rodeo was the perfect end to the one real cowboy week of the year, even if we were sitting on wet bleachers shivering and watching men ride broncs and rope calves in ankle-deep mud.

With Jill, in 1949, before
she gave birth to Jack.

[12]

Jack and Jill

M Y FATHER SURRENDERED to my horse ownership ambitions more or less by accident. He bought a three-year-old mare at the weekly livestock auction in Gothenburg. Dad's hostility to cowboying had begun to soften, possibly because we were now a little more prosperous, but also because our cowboy heritage had taken on a slightly more favorable light. As we began to have more contact with the outside world, it became apparent that the only aspect of life in our world that was the least bit interesting to outsiders was the cowboy angle. Tourists came to the rodeo, town people liked to take part in branding, and all the neighboring towns liked to have us dress western and ride horses in their parades. It was hard to resist being what people wanted us to be.

Dad said he bought the mare on an impulse, because he liked her calm demeanor when she was ridden into the auction ring. That in itself revealed a seismic shift in Dad, because he was not an impulsive man. He hauled her home in our Model AA truck and unloaded her on a pile of corn cobs. She didn't get spooked even sliding down among the loose cobs, confirming Dad's instinct about her disposition.

Her name was Jill. She was barely broke to ride, but she was gentle and sensible. Dad had bought her to ride himself, but he let me ride her too. I was too short to reach her head, but she would obligingly lower it to let me slip the bridle on—a miraculous concession, because most horses hate the bridle more than the saddle. To get Dad's heavy saddle on her, I had to lug the saddle to a feed bunk and get Jill to stand beside the bunk while I climbed onto it and threw the saddle on her back. As with the bridle, she seemed perfectly willing to help me out by standing close to the bunk.

That Christmas I got my own saddle. When we opened our presents on Christmas Eve I didn't get anything noteworthy, so when Dad asked me to go to the barn to see if he had forgotten to turn off the light, I knew I would find my present there. When I opened the door, there it was, hanging from a rafter. It was a saddle any boy would die for—not a kid saddle but a youth model with a 13-inch seat, made by the legendary Texas saddlemaker Buck Steiner, every surface except the seat covered with a hand-stamped floral design. It was Steiner's famous Little Wonder design, with swells and narrow, leather-wrapped stirrups—a style you could use on a horse that might buck.

Dad had bought it secondhand from Lundin's Saddle Shop in Brady. We later learned that it had belonged to Roger Booth, who had traded it in on a new full-size saddle. But I didn't recognize it as my cousin's, and that didn't matter to me anyway, because it was a saddle that would make any boy look good. Now my only problem was that I had a horse to ride only if Dad didn't need Jill, and that meant I still might end up afoot at branding time or any other time when there was real horseback work to be done. But as it turned out, Jill had a solution to that problem.

It rained the night before my tenth birthday, so we took the day off and went to the Memorial Day horse races at the county fairgrounds in Broken Bow. They weren't big-time races by any means, just ranchers putting their fastest horses up against their neighbors' best. There was no pari-mutuel betting, of course, but there was lots of wagering in the grandstand. The track was a mud bath for horses and riders alike. Still, they were the first organized horse races I had seen, and as we drove the fifty miles home I was tired and happy.

As we approached our place, driving beside the lane that led to our milk cow pasture, there among the trees was Jill with a newborn foal. It was barely able to stand, but it was a beautiful baby, a slightly lighter shade of sorrel than Jill, with a white star in its forehead and white socks on its front legs.

"I guess Jill wanted you to have a birthday present," Dad said. He hadn't known Jill was pregnant when he bought her, but realized it a few months before she gave birth, and decided to let the foal come as a surprise to me. And surprise it was, to both of us. Dad hadn't dreamed it would come on my birthday, and I couldn't have been more surprised if the foal had dropped from heaven before my eyes. It was the happiest day of my life.

The next day we determined that it was male. I wanted to name him Lightning, but Dad thought a son of Jill had to be named Jack. I called him Lightning for a while, but with everybody else in the family calling him Jack I soon gave in.

I had a halter on him within a few days. He didn't have Jill's obliging disposition, but that was okay; I didn't want a horse who would steal my opportunity to break him myself.

I don't know why we and everyone else in the West used the term "break." No one I knew threw a saddle on a wild horse and rode it till it quit bucking. Our methods were closer to those of the Horse Whisperer. Even when Jack was only a few weeks old, he was too strong for me to manhandle. I broke him to lead by getting the halter on him, turning Jill out to pasture, and then trotting along with him, holding the lead rope as he followed her. Before he was a year old I got him used to having a saddle blanket on his back. It never scared him and he never resisted it. After he got a little bigger I eased up onto his back and just sat there, bareback.

The only step he didn't like was being saddled. I was too short to be able to ease the saddle onto his back: I had to wind up and swing it as high as I could reach. He jumped out from under the saddle a few times, but soon he got used to it and just stiffened when the stirrups and straps slapped against his sides. By the time he was big enough to ride, the only thing new to him was having the saddle and me on his back at the same time. He bucked a jump or two the first few times I started him trotting or loping in an open area, but that was just friskiness, not a serious effort to get me off. I loved the hours of patient coaxing and reassuring, and each advance produced a moment of triumphant happiness.

While Jack was growing up, I still rode Jill, often with Jack tagging along at her flank. Now that I had a fabulous saddle and horse-to-be of my own, I was the equal of anyone, even Joe Tetro. One day I rode Jill the two miles to the Tetros, just to show off to Joe. When I got ready to leave, one of us challenged the other to a race: Joe would take a short cut to their mailbox on foot, and Jill and I, with Jack trailing along, would take the longer route out the driveway and back up the road to the mailbox. Unfortunately, there was a muddy spot where the driveway met the road, and as I made the sharp right turn at a dead run, Jill's feet hit the mud and she came down hard on her side.

I wasn't hurt, but Jill got up favoring a hind leg, and soon there was a swelling on her hip. In a week or so the swelling went down and she stopped limping, but then her milk dried up. So Jack was weaned prematurely and had to learn to eat grain before he was quite ready. It didn't affect his growth, and Jill suffered no visible long-term effects, but she was never quite as lively after that. And I was never quite as reckless with horses. I had begun to understand that acts have consequences.

By the time Jack was a two-year-old, I was riding him in the roundups and at every other opportunity. In the summers a girl named Rose came to visit our neighbors to the east, the Raetzes. They had a big jugheaded plow horse that Rose loved to ride. She often rode over to our place to see if I could go riding with her. If I wasn't working, I did. We usually rode down the gulch toward the river, practicing reining our horses in figure-eights, jumping across gullies, exhilarating in the freedom of galloping across the native grass of the plains.

But the world was too much with us. Rose was a big girl, half again my size, and her horse was a disgrace. When Joe Tetro found out I went riding with her, he ridiculed me mercilessly. Other neighbors saw us riding and teased me about my "girlfriend." I began making excuses when Rose showed up to ride. I can still see her standing with her horse in our yard, bewilderment in her face and disappointment in the sag of her shoulders when I told her once again I couldn't go.

Horses were our major source of pleasure but also a constant danger. I first learned that bones could break when Roger Booth got bucked off his pony and broke his arm. Our neighbor Hank Gustafson, father of my first teacher, was run over by a team and wagon and was crippled for the rest of his life.

After I was grown, my father suffered the same fate when a horse fell and crushed his leg. He was rounding up cattle one April morning on a new quarter horse named Johnny. As he was driving the cows down a shallow canyon toward the corrals, one cow broke from the herd and darted up the hillside. Johnny eagerly charged after her, but his feet hit a patch of lingering ice. Johnny came down hard on his side, with Dad's leg beneath him.

The leg was badly crushed, with several nasty fractures of the tibia and fibula. The horse was unhurt and went straight home, but Mother was not at home so the riderless horse set off no alarms. Dad lay helpless on the icy ground for several hours, miles from the nearest town and several hundred yards from the nearest dirt road. It may have been the cold that saved him: sound carries a long way on cold quiet morning air, and eventually a neighbor arrived home, half a mile away, and heard Dad's weakening calls for help.

The leg was crudely patched up by a local general practitioner, and Dad was never again able to ride a horse or walk normally.

I've lost consciousness twice in my life, both times in horse accidents. When I was eleven or twelve and breaking my colt Jack, he kicked me squarely in the solar plexus. I was (and still am) proud of the poise I showed in the situation. I didn't let go of the reins, and although I was unable to breathe, I led Jack thirty yards to the barn, tied him up and walked to the house, still not breathing. That was a dumb thing to do, of course. I regained consciousness a few minutes later on the kitchen floor, with my mother crying, "What's the matter? What happened?"

A year or two later I was riding Jack while we rounded up cattle. We came over the top of a long hill leading to the corrals. The next thing I remember is lying in the grass at the bottom of the hill with somebody slapping my face and asking if I was okay.

"What happened?" I asked.

"Your horse fell."

"How did I get to the bottom of the hill?"

"That's where he fell."

Apparently my head hit the ground when the horse fell, and the blow obliterated my memory of the preceding few minutes.

These are accidents that can happen even if the horse is a perfectly sensible animal and you've done nothing foolhardy. But there are evil-hearted horses, too, and they're even more hazardous. My friend Keith Blackledge was taking newspaper photos at a rodeo when a bucking horse cornered him in the roping box and knocked out a few of his teeth. For the next fifty years, Keith flashed some handsome gold teeth.

About the time Jack was old enough to ride, for my twelfth birthday I got a .22 rifle, a Winchester bolt-action single-shot. I wasn't a very good shot, possibly because my eyesight was poor and I refused to wear glasses, but I felt like I was finally complete. I had a horse, a saddle, and a gun—all a cowboy needed, according to the myth.

I began plotting to be a real-life Lone Ranger. I would disappear into the south hills and become the mystery man, occasionally seen riding my horse on a high ridge in the distance, never allowing myself to be caught or identified. I knew the hills and canyons extended all the way to the Republican River, sixty miles to the south, with only scattered human habitation. I would live off the land, killing game, picking wild fruit, taking shelter in abandoned buildings when weather was bad. If I had to slip into someone's house to take a can of beans, I would leave a pheasant or a rabbit as payment.

I found the date of the full moon in June and chose that as my date of departure. I gathered what I would need: a few boxes of .22 shells, a pair of fence pinchers so I could let down fences and put them back up as I moved across the pastures, a waterproof jacket and some gloves, an extra saddle blanket to sleep on, and a small mirror so I could use the sun to signal people far away, to make them notice me before I galloped away down the far side of the ridge. I stashed everything in the barn.

When the night of the full moon came, I lay awake in my bed for a long time, waiting to be sure my parents were asleep. I tiptoed downstairs and didn't put on my boots until I got outside. I saddled Jack in the dark, strapped my gear to the saddle, and started off toward the canyons I knew from our roundups.

It turned out to be one of those plains nights when a balmy breeze suddenly and inexplicably turns into a chilly wind. When I started, the moon was bright and I could see as if it were day. There were clouds, though, and when they moved across the moon I was surprised at how dark it got. As I got closer to the hills, it seemed to get even darker and colder. The hills and canyons, which looked inviting by day, now looked foreboding. I began shivering—from the chill, I think.

At the mouth of the canyon, I had one of those moments when rationalization masquerades as inspiration: this was just the wrong night! I could turn back, and it wouldn't mean I was never going; I would just wait for a better night! So I turned around, rode home, unsaddled Jack, and tiptoed back to bed. But when I got in bed, it felt so safe and warm that I knew I would never be the mystery man of the hills.

After a couple more years, Jill got a bad barbed wire cut on a foot. It wouldn't heal properly, so we finally sent her off to the slaughterhouse. That was a painful day, worse for Dad than me, I think. I still had Jack, but for Dad, Jill had been a case of love at first sight.

During World War II Dad picked our
corn himself. This is a photo of Nancy
and me with him on a load of corn.
After the war, Dad hired Norm and Rufus
to do the picking, using rigs like this.

[13]

Norm and Rufus

IN THE BLEAKNESS OF WINTER ON THE PLAINS, my favorite place was the bunkhouse of Norm and Rufus, my first grown-up friends. They were itinerant farm hands who came to our place every fall in the late '40s to pick our corn. In an otherwise sterile winter world, where the only things that varied were the velocity of the wind and the shades of gray in the landscape, the bunkhouse was a sensory banquet.

It was a teardrop-shaped trailer house, wood-framed and covered with silver rubberized fabric like the skin of prewar airplanes. The interior glistened with thick varnish and the wind rattled the fabric. It was crowded, cozy, and always too warm; men who work in the cold all day never get too much heat. It smelled of propane heat, sweat, leather, wet clothes drying, Woolfat, flatulence, and lots of tobacco—stale tobacco, chewing tobacco, and fresh tobacco smoke.

Norm had been a Marine in World War II, but he looked like he should have been in the Navy. He was of medium height, slight but broad-shouldered, and he walked with an unsteady swagger, like a sailor just arrived in port. His mannerisms were boyish and he looked to be in his early twenties. He had pale blue eyes, reddish-blond hair, and fine clean features. He looked a little like Alan Ladd.

Norm always looked slightly out of kilter. One side of his face was a little longer than the other, making his chin and his smile slightly off-center. He was left-handed and he moved as lefties in a right-handed world often do—uncertainly, as if he weren't quite sure which way to turn, how to stand, what to say. He wasn't exactly happy-go-lucky, but neither was he fierce or moody or mean, as the movies had led us to expect Marines to be. He looked as if he always expected something good to happen, even if it never did.

Norm was shyly polite around women and they adored him. They always wanted to do something for him—feed him, mend his clothes, or tend his everyday nicks and cuts. Mother's solicitude for Norm irritated Dad, though he tried to act merely bemused by it.

Rufus was older, probably in his late thirties. He was tall with narrow shoulders and thick wrists. His belly was so perfectly round he appeared to have swallowed a basketball. He had dark hair, dark close-set eyes, big ears, a thick nose, loose jowls, and a coarse stubble that didn't seem to go away even when he shaved. But at first you didn't notice those things: you only noticed the thick dark tufts of hair that grew out of his nostrils and ears.

Rufus had been 4-F in the war for reasons I never heard mentioned, but which in retrospect are obvious enough. He had the most frightening cough I've ever heard. He would rumble, wheeze, strangle, and curse for an agonizingly long time, then spit a puddle of reddish brown phlegm. He rarely spoke, but his cough punctuated the conversation; everyone else had to stop talking and wait for Rufus to stop coughing. I suppose he could have had tuberculosis, though I don't remember anyone mentioning that possibility at the time.

Sometimes Rufus would be too tired to go to town on Saturday night, and some Sundays he would spend most of the day in bed. The last year or two I recall Mother and Dad discussing with Norm whether Rufus was well enough to go on picking corn. Norm said Rufus wanted to keep working, so he did.

Norm and Rufus moved as a team from one farm job to another. They were dependable and good workers, so they returned to the same farms year after year, to one place for wheat harvest, another for haying season, another to dig potatoes, and to our place to pick corn. Sometimes they stayed on to pick corn for others in the community after ours was finished.

Many men had lived like that in our part of the country during the Depression when there were no permanent jobs to be had, but after the war it was unusual. Norm and Rufus were holdovers from that long period in American history when, in John Neihardt's phrase, "men were cheaper than money." The West was built by men like them—miners and cowboys and railroad builders—whose work consisted mostly of drudgery, danger, and loneliness, and whose pleasures were a warm place to sleep, a full stomach, a paycheck, tobacco, liquor, and perhaps an occasional paid woman.

Many of these men were used up by the work, killed or worn out. Others were simply cast aside when their labor was no longer needed; that was to be the fate of Norm and Rufus, although I didn't suspect it at the time.

After supper and on Sunday afternoons, I hung out with Norm and Rufus in their trailer. It had a bed in the back, a closet and some cabinets in the middle, and the rudiments of a kitchen—an icebox, a hot plate, a dishpan, and a linoleum-covered table with benches on either side—in the front. Everything was built-in, made of plywood, and a little too small. The trailer was parked close behind our house so an extension cord would reach to provide electricity. It was between two rows of cedar trees that blocked maybe five per cent of the wind, and convenient to the outhouse that we all shared.

The table and benches at the front of the trailer could be re-arranged to make a second bed but I never saw it made up. Norm and Rufus obviously shared the bed in the back. None of us found that the least bit remarkable, maybe because it never occurred to us that two men in a bed might do anything but sleep. Or maybe we just found it convenient to be tolerant.

There was no running water in the trailer, so if Norm or Rufus bathed, they must have done so in a galvanized metal washtub in our kitchen, as the rest of us did. When I asked my father many years later where Norm and Rufus bathed, he said, only half-joking, "Bathe? It was wintertime." It was an era when people really did bathe "once a week in summer, not quite so often in winter."

Norm usually sat at the table smoking and playing solitaire. He had a cheap radio, tuned to whatever would come in: a faith healer on the Clear Channel station in Clint ("that's C-L-I-N-T"), Texas; Fibber Mc-Gee and Molly; Joe diNatale announcing a high school basketball game on KODY in North Platte; or Guy Lombardo on WWL in New Orleans.

Norm could roll a cigarette with one hand while he played cards with the other. With his left hand he would fish in his shirt pocket for the little orange-covered packet of cigarette papers, pull one out and lay it on the table, pull the little cloth bag of Bull Durham from his pocket, and open it with his teeth. He could shake out just the right amount of tobacco without looking and close the bag by pulling the paper tag at the end of the drawstring with his teeth. Then he put the bag away, picked up the cigarette paper with his thumb and middle finger, leveled the tobacco with his forefinger, licked the edge of the paper once on the inside to make it sticky, and ran his tongue back the other way to fold the paper over the tobacco.

Still without looking, he would put one end of the cigarette in his mouth, twist the other to keep the tobacco from falling out, pull a match from the bundle of kitchen matches he kept in his shirt pocket, and strike it on his shoe. He didn't take his eyes off the cards until he lighted the cigarette; then he would tilt his head back so the brief flare-up of the twisted paper at the end didn't singe his eyebrows, take a couple of deep drags to get the tobacco burning, shake out the match and break it in two before throwing it away.

Watching this, any kid would be tempted to smoke just to see if he could master the ritual. I tried, then and later, to roll cigarettes one-handed, but I could never get it down. How a working man with thick, cracked, calloused fingers could have such dexterity baffles me still.

Once Norm got the cigarette lit it stayed in his mouth. It stuck to his lower lip while he talked, bobbing up and down while he squinted to keep the acrid blue smoke out of his eyes. If ashes fell on the table or his clothes he brushed them onto the floor.

Rufus lay on the bed and smoked Prince Albert, which came in a tall red can flat enough to fit in a shirt pocket. He sometimes smoked it in a corncob pipe, but usually he rolled a cigarette. When the cans were empty he gave them to me. They made great containers for pennies, marbles, and bugs. When Rufus wasn't smoking he chewed Red Man; I suppose that is what made his spit reddish-brown instead of blood red. He let me try a plug once; it was stringy and bitter and I gagged.

"See there," he said, "like I told you, it's a dirty habit. Don't get started. Smoke if you want to, but don't chaw."

Norm or Rufus gave me a drag on their cigarettes now and then. "Don't tell your ma," Norm said, "we'll both git skinned."

Norm called me Davy. I hated it when others called me that, but it was okay coming from Norm because he had a nickname for everybody. He called most men and kids "Pal." He called all women "Ma'am."

I suppose Norm and Rufus let me hang around because I was somebody new to talk to. They didn't have much to say to each other that the other didn't already know. When they did talk between themselves, it was often over my head. For example, they sometimes kidded each other about "going to the Platte" when the corn was out. Everybody called the town of North Platte "the Platte" and most people went there a few times a year to the rodeo or to do business at the courthouse or to buy school clothes. I didn't see why the prospect of going there made them so playful.

Now I think I know. North Platte at that time had open prostitution. Women in cheap hotels and rooming houses along Front Street served the railroaders and ranch hands just as they had since the days of the frontier. My friend Keith Blackledge, long-time editor of the *North Platte Telegraph,* told me it finally ended in 1951 when people of the town became aware that high school boys were patronizing the whorehouses. Indignant citizens got together a reform slate and voted out the officials who had allowed North Platte to be "wide open."

What I really wanted to hear Norm talk about was the war. Most of my curiosity arose from the movies that were made after the war (or maybe were made during the war but only reached us later). The real war had had little direct impact on us. The only war memory I have is of squadrons of fighters and bombers, flying in formation, so high they were barely visible but in such numbers that the sky would gradually fill with a harmonic drone so intense that it seemed to be trying to drill into my head. In the first years of the war they were eastbound—flying from the factories in California to Europe, people said. In later years they were westbound, and people said they were headed for Japan.

Norm had joined the Marines early in the war and fought across the Pacific. I can't remember exactly where he fought. Names like

Okinawa, Guam, Guadalcanal, and Iwo Jima spring from memory, but I'm not sure whether I first heard them from Norm or the movies. But I knew that Norm was a real-life hero and had been to the places and seen the things that the movies showed. I pestered him constantly to tell me about the war.

"Did you kill any Japs, Norm? Did they live in caves? Did you burn 'em out? How come you won't talk about it? Did you ever kill one with your bare hands?"

"Where did you ever get those ideas?" Norm asked.

"I seen it at the show."

"It wasn't like it is in the picture show."

"Did you ever see anybody get killed?"

"Yeah, I seen some."

"Did you get shot at? Did you shoot back?"

Usually Norm would find some excuse to leave: "Better see what those clouds are doin'" or "I gotta take a leak."

Sometimes Rufus would speak up. "Leave Norm alone, kid. He don't like to talk about it."

Once I heard Rufus tell someone that Norm had nightmares about dead Japs. Sometimes Norm would mention "a buddy I had on Iwo." But I never got him to tell me the things I yearned to know: Was he scared? If he killed a Jap, did it make him feel bad? Do dead men bleed?

Some things he *would* talk about.

"Do they have palm trees over there?"

"I never seen any. All I seen is rocks and beach."

"Did you ever get seasick?"

"Damn right I did. We all did. First day or two out of San Diego, everything was pretty and blue. Then a couple days out, it turned windy and commenced to rain. Ship was bobbin' around like a tin can. Guys was pukin' everywhere. If the waves didn't make you sick, the sight of all that puke did. I didn't eat nuthin all the way to Hawaii. When we got there we was all too weak to go see the place."

People kidded Norm about girls.

"How come a good-lookin' feller like you ain't got him a girl-friend?"

"You go to town all slicked up like that, some girl's gonna latch onto you and not let you come back."

Norm would blush and squirm. "Ain't ready to settle down yet."

People kidded me about girls too, so I sympathized with him and didn't ask him much about that. Once, though, he told me he had a girlfriend back in O'Neill before the war.

"Then how come you don't go back and get her?" I asked.

"'Cause she ain't there no more." He looked unhappy, so I didn't ask where she went.

Later Rufus told me that Norm's girl took up with another guy while Norm was in the service.

At one time all corn was picked by hand, but just before the war mechanical corn-pickers became available and a few farmers bought them. Once the war started it was impossible to buy any new machinery. During the war many farmers, including my father, picked their own corn because neither machines nor human pickers were available. In the war years farmers harvested abundant crops that brought good prices. As soon as the factories returned to civilian production after the war, farmers eagerly spent their money on new machinery. Those who didn't have their own mechanical corn-pickers paid a farmer who did to bring his machine and pick their corn.

We were among the last holdouts. Dad and a few other farmers thought the machines missed too many ears of corn, so we kept our team of work horses for corn-picking even after we had switched to tractors for everything else. Throughout the late '40s we hired Norm and Rufus to pick our corn the old-fashioned way.

Good corn-pickers like Norm and Rufus could shuck as much as a hundred bushels each—two or three wagonloads—on a good day, though sixty or seventy bushels was probably more typical. They could snap even more, because of the time saved by not removing the husk. They made seven or eight cents a bushel, plus room and board. We furnished the teams and wagons. If they stayed healthy and the weather cooperated and the corn was thick, they could earn twice as much in a day as ordinary farm and ranch hands made.

Corn-picking season was late fall. It couldn't begin until a hard frost killed the stalks and a few weeks of dry weather dried out the kernels. If the corn was picked too soon, internal moisture would cause it to spoil or even spontaneously catch fire when it was stored. Corn-picking was necessarily done in the cold, and often in the snow. If frost came early and the fall stayed dry, picking could begin by late October. But a warm wet fall could postpone the start until late November, and then blizzards or wet snow might drag it on into January or February.

Norm and Rufus harnessed their teams and hitched up their wagons in predawn darkness. They began picking as soon as it was light enough to see the ears on the stalks, and often unloaded the last wagon after dark. They wore bib overalls over longjohns, four-buckle rubber overshoes, flannel or denim shirts, and corduroy or plaid flannel caps with ear flaps. They started the day wearing heavy jackets, even sheepskin coats if it was really cold, but soon shed those in the heat of work. In the morning the corn was covered with frost, which soon soaked their mittens. They wore cheap cotton mittens made with a thumb on either side, so when the palm wore out they could turn the mitten around and wear it until that side wore out too.

The cold and wet, and the constant abrasion of the hard, rough ears, were cruel to hands. A corn-picker's hands were always red, cal-lused, cracked, swollen, and sore. They treated them with the same medication we used for chapped lips and cracked cow's udders: Wool-fat. Woolfat was literally that—a paste made from oils and lanolin pressed out of wool. It came from the drugstore in a square tin and smelled bad, but it worked as well as any ointment I've seen since. In the evenings Norm and Rufus worked Woolfat into the cracks and calluses of their hands, and often their lips and ears because the relentless wind abused those too.

I was crazy about Norm and Rufus. They were men who knew adventure, travel, freedom, even danger. Norm was the only person I knew who had seen an ocean, let alone crossed it and seen foreign lands. Everybody else I knew lived in one place, in a family and a com-munity. Norm and Rufus were the first people I knew who were *different*. Even though they came back year after year, ate three meals a day at our table, went to town with us on Saturday night, and whiled away Sunday afternoons with us, they were mysterious strangers. I assumed they would be part of our lives forever, like Sunday school or summer. But of course that was not to be.

[14]

A Desperate Life

MY FATHER YIELDED TO MECHANIZATION a few years after the war. The Depression-born impulse to gather every last ear of corn gave way to the post-war ideology of plenty: if the machine enables you to harvest ten percent more acres, it doesn't matter that it wastes five percent. So we hired a neighbor to pick the corn with his machine, and we didn't need Norm and Rufus anymore. We didn't see either of them for several years.

During that period, we moved away from the Union community. It was time for me to go to high school. No school bus came out as far as our farm, so I would have had to drive myself to town every day or board in town. Driving wasn't a practical option because the roads were often impassable. There were relatives in town that I could have boarded with, but I had three younger sisters; before long, more of the family would have been boarding in town than living at home.

So we bought a farm just a mile west of Gothenburg, close enough that all of us could walk to town school. It's obvious now that Union School and the community were both in jeopardy if every family was going to leave when the eldest child finished the eighth grade, but so far as I can recall, we never gave that a thought. We were all going to have the benefit of town school, and equally importantly, the opportunity to participate in after-school activities like band and sports.

We moved in the summer of 1952, and late that year Dad got a letter from Norm. He was down on his luck and needed work. No one hired corn-pickers any more, and there wasn't any other farm work to be done at that time of year. He didn't say anything about Rufus.

We had kept the lease on our old farm at Union and Dad was

planning to winter the cattle there in the picked-over cornfields—
letting the cattle feed on the five percent of the corn that the machine
missed. He wrote Norm back and offered him a job for the winter
looking after the cattle. Norm was a corn-picker, not a cowboy, but
Dad figured he could chop holes in the ice on the water tanks, haul hay
to the cattle, and keep an eye on the cows that were about to calve.

Norm didn't bother to mail a reply. Within a couple of days he
showed up at our door ready to go to work. "I don't know nothin' about
cows, Arnold, but you know I'm a worker. You tell me what to do, I'll
do 'er."

Dad warned him, "It's a damned lonesome job, out there with
nothin' but the wind and the cows."

"That's okay, it's more'n I got now."

If that was true, Norm's life really had reached bottom. The job
was inhumanly lonesome. Norm lived in the old farmhouse we had
abandoned, thirteen miles from Gothenburg. That homely old house
was desolate in winter even when it was filled with a lively family. On
the utterly flat plain of the Platte Valley it stood tall and gangly, three
rooms down and four up, with tall narrow windows, a steep roof, and
no decoration except the lightning rods on the peak of the roof.

There was no insulation in the walls. When we lived there the
doors and windows on the north were sealed over in winter with
isinglass, but I doubt any had been installed the winter Norm was
there because we hadn't expected anybody to be living there. Without
it, the walls and windows would have done little more than carve the
steady roar of the north wind into shrieks and whistles. If there was
any furniture in the house, it probably wasn't more than a cot and a
kitchen range. Maybe there was a little coal left over from the previous
winter; if not, Norm would have had no fuel except corn cobs.

Norm had no car. Dad drove out once a week or so and brought
Norm back to town. He would leave Norm off at the grocery store, pick
him up a few hours later at the beer joint, and drive him back to the old
farmhouse.

Sometimes Norm would have a meal with us while he was in
town. On one visit I showed him a stripped-down Model A Ford we had

inherited when we bought the farm. The front end of the body and the chassis were intact, but the rear half of the body had been cut off. All that remained from the windshield back were the floor and the front seat. It didn't run, but I had dreams of fixing it up and mounting a sleek sports car body on it.

Norm also had designs on the Ford. "Arnold, would you mind if I tinkered a little with that flivver? If I could git it goin' I could drive it out there to the place and you wouldn't have to be runnin' me back and forth."

Dad said okay. Norm borrowed a pair of pliers, some wire, a screwdriver, and a little gas, and in an hour or two he had the Model A running. When he proposed to drive it home, we all thought he was crazy.

"Norm, you'll freeze to death," Mother said.

'It's close to dark and you've got no lights," Dad said.

"Don't worry about me, I'll have this baby home in no time," Norm said. He pulled the ear flaps down on his cap, clapped his mittened hands together a couple of times, hopped onto the bare springs of the seat, and chugged off into the icy twilight.

A couple of weeks later we heard an "ooogaah" in the yard. It was Norm, and the flivver now had a body. He had built a box-shaped cab— a wooden frame covered with cardboard and attached with wire to the windshield and the floor. In the back was a flap of old canvas so he could crawl in and out. The driver's side had a peep hole covered with a piece of cellophane. An old blanket covered the seat springs.

"Snug as a Cadillac," he said. "Looky here." He pointed to the floorboard, where he had cut a hole and bent a piece of tin to deflect heat from the exhaust manifold back into the cab.

We shook our heads and marveled at Norm's ingenuity. Mother said, "Henry Ford's got nothin' on you, Norm."

Norm stayed for supper, but as soon as it was over he excused himself. "Long way home," he said. "I'm startin' to git attached to them old cows. Can't hardly stand to leave 'em."

We laughed, and he drove off in the dark. Dad said, "It'll be a long way home by the time he gets there, all right. He'll be at the beer joint till they throw him out."

A couple of weeks later Dad got a phone call early Sunday morning.

"Yeah. . . . He works for us. . . . Oh no. . . . Okay, I'll be there quick as I can."

Dad looked grim when he hung up. I knew Norm was in trouble, and he wasn't in the hospital because Dad hadn't asked, "How is he?"

Dad was gone most of the morning. When he got home he didn't want to talk and he didn't need to, because we all knew what had happened: Norm had got drunk and ended up in jail, and Dad had got him out.

I never knew exactly why Norm got arrested. There were always drunks on Front Street in Gothenburg on Saturday night and they didn't seem to get arrested. I assumed Norm either passed out or got in a fight.

Although I hoped otherwise, I knew in my heart that Norm's days with us were numbered. Dad had no sympathy for drinkers. He had adored his older brother August, but Uncle Augie's drinking cost him his job, his wife, and eventually his life, and Dad never forgave him. In Dad's mind anyone who drank was bound to become a drunk. There was no such thing as a good man who occasionally drank too much.

For Norm, the string played out on a snowy weekend a few weeks later. On Sunday evening the phone rang. It was for Dad. I could tell it was Norm. He had no phone at the farmhouse, so he must have gone to a neighbor's.

The conversation was short. When it ended, Dad said, "He lost a pair of twin bull calves. Goddamn him! I told him!"

It was late February. There was snow on the ground, and over the weekend it had turned bitterly cold. Most cattlemen in our part of the country bred their cows to begin calving in March, but Dad liked to have extra big calves at weaning time in the fall. He turned his bulls into the pastures earlier so the calves began to drop around Valentine's Day. That meant they often came in the worst weather of winter, so the cows and the weather had to be watched closely.

Usually nature worked just fine and all the cow and calf needed was a place where the calf wouldn't freeze to death before the cow could lick it dry and persuade it to stand up and nurse. But sometimes calves got stuck in the birth canal and had to be pulled. Sometimes the newborn calf was too weak to nurse; sometimes a cow would inexplicably refuse to let her calf nurse. Occasionally it was so cold that the calf had to be brought into the house and warmed beside the kitchen stove for a few hours before being returned to the cow.

Dad generally knew how long it would be before a cow gave birth. He could tell it from her behavior. He could predict the weather, at least in the short term, from the look of the sky and the feel of the wind.

"This one'll calve by this time tomorrow, but I don't think she'll do it tonight. It may storm tomorrow, but not tonight. We can leave her out now but we'll have to get her in first thing in the morning."

Norm wasn't a cattleman. He had failed to get the cow in soon enough and she calved out in the mud and snow. The cow was a good one; she had produced some of our very best calves. She was bred that year to a new bull and Dad was eager to see the result.

Dad went to the old farm the next day, and when he came back he looked sick. I wanted to ask about Norm, but all of us could see that Dad didn't want to talk. When he finally did, despair and anger spilled out together.

"Prettiest pair of bull calves you ever seen. Backs a foot wide and flat as a board. Big devils, you wouldn't know they was twins. Neither one of 'em ever got up. It was too damn cold. They just laid out there in the snow and froze to death."

I thought Dad might cry. Instead his voice rose and his face contorted in pain and anger.

"That goddamn Norm. Said he checked 'em all late Saturday and first thing Sunday. He didn't, I know he didn't. I know damned well he was off in the goddamn beer joint. "I told him when I got him outta jail, 'If you don't cut out this drinkin', you're through. I won't put up with it.' He said he wouldn't drink no more, couldn't afford to lose this job. Thanked me over and over again for gettin' him outta jail. 'You'll never have to do this again, I promise. I've learnt my lesson, won't touch the stuff.' He's a liar. Goddamn good-for-nothin' drunk."

The tirade seemed to deflate Dad. He looked defeated, crushed. He put on his coat and went outside.

Later Mother asked quietly, "Is Norm still out there?"

"I paid him off," Dad said. "Told him he's finished. Brought him back to town and let him out at the bus depot. I imagine he headed straight for the beer joint."

We never saw Norm again. A year or two later he wrote at Christmas time. He said he always liked working for us and missed us. He didn't say where he was working, only that he was "doing a little of this and a little of that." Rufus had died. He missed Rufus too. He hoped we remembered the old times.

At the end he wrote, in his left-handed slant, "Tell Davy I said hi. Your pal, Norm."

This is Dad when he was named
Nebraska Hereford Man of the Year.

[15]

Cattleman

AFTER THE TWO-DAY CATTLE DRIVE from Maywood, which I described in an earlier chapter, we were one cow short when we arrived at the summer pastures. Dad quickly determined that the missing cow was a three-year-old that had not yet calved, and he surmised that the long walk had induced labor. The next day he took a trailer and quickly found the hiding place of the heifer and her newborn calf, twelve or fifteen miles back along our route.

"I just looked for a place that would look good to a tired cow about to have a calf," he said. "She was back in a little canyon, up against a sunny bank in a clump of bushes. She had a good healthy bull calf."

That was typical of my father's cow sense. He knew cattle the way a horseman knows horses. He appreciated their personalities, understood their minds, sensed their emotions, and knew their habits.

It may seem inevitable that a cattleman would understand cattle, but in fact most don't. They only know them in the aggregate—things like acres of pasture required per cow-calf unit, daily rate of gain, calving percentages, and price per hundredweight. They know cattle the way a commodities trader knows wheat.

Dad understood them as individuals. To him no two were alike. They were as different—and as similar—as people. Some would break for freedom at the slightest opportunity; others wouldn't dream of leaving the herd. Some could be trusted to look after themselves and their offspring in almost any circumstance; others could be trusted only to get themselves in trouble. Anyone who is around cattle will learn those things in general, of course, but Dad knew what each particular cow was likely to do. It was as if he could read their minds.

In summer his cows ran in herds of forty to fifty cows with calves, and one bull, in pastures of two hundred to three hundred acres. They were hilly pastures, sculpted with high ridges, canyons, and pockets filled with brush and small trees. A man on horseback could easily spend half a day finding all of the cattle in one pasture and getting them in a corral where he could count them. Dad could drive into the pasture in a pickup, find the main herd, count them as they grazed, and identify the missing individuals. Then, by factoring in the weather, the time of day, the quality of the grass and water, and the personalities of the missing, he usually could go straight to them.

I never saw him rope from horseback, but on foot he was deadly efficient with a lariat. He never twirled the rope overhead as cowboys do—that scares the cattle. He moved quietly among them, keeping the rope low and out of sight, looking for the one that needed pink-eye medicine or new horn weights. He would wait until he had the right angle. If you're on foot and you rope a cow when she's running away from you, there's no way you can hold her; a well-fed Hereford cow weighs well over half a ton. But if you rope her while she's facing you and pull the rope tight before she can turn, she can only back away. Cattle can't back very fast or very far. If the cow isn't too wild—and ours weren't—she will soon give up and let you ease up the rope to her head. If she doesn't, you just hope she will drag you close to a fence post or tree so you can take a quick wrap and hold her.

Most of our cattle were used to being roped and they understood the game. They would try to duck out from under the loop, and when that failed they would fight for a few seconds. Then they would stand, straining against the rope but not fighting. Usually there was one more brief fight when the medicine hit the eye or the weight was tightened onto the horn, then sullen surrender. Dad would then finish his work, talking calmly all the while:

"What's the matter, momma? That stuff sting? It's okay, momma, you got a bad eye there and this's gonna make it better."

Or, if he had less sympathy for the patient:

"Stand still, you goddamn old bitch. If you wasn't so damn stupid you wouldn't get yourself hurt all the time."

When he finished he would rub the cow's neck for a minute, still talking softly. Then in one instant he would release the tension on the rope and jerk the loop free from the cow's head and horns. This was the trickiest part of the whole operation. The second the cow feels the rope loosen she throws up her head and tries to run. If you don't get the loop off cleanly you find yourself being towed behind a cow with a full head of steam. That happened to me once or twice, but I never saw it happen to Dad.

After being handled this way two or three times, most of Dad's cattle had little fear of him or the rope. He could walk up to some of them and throw a rope on them in a three-hundred-acre pasture. Of course, he also knew which ones *not* to rope when there was nothing to snub to.

Dad had a special technique for roping cattle in a crowded corral. With thirty frightened yearlings swirling past in a bawling mass, Dad could snake his loop out over the upraised heads and drop it on the one he wanted. When the victim felt the rope it would instinctively drop its head and stop, trying to back out. Dad wouldn't pull the rope tight immediately because he had to let the rest of the herd run under it. So he would hold the slack high, like a fisherman playing out line. In a second or two the interlopers would flash past and he would be face to face with the yearling he wanted.

This is a whole lot easier to describe than to do. There are a lot of possibilities, and most of them are bad: You don't catch anything. You catch the wrong one. You catch two in one loop. You catch only one but it gets through the loop before you get a chance to pull the slack and you have a yearling by one hind foot in a pen of frantic yearlings. You catch the one you want (or one you didn't want) by the head but others get tangled up in your rope.

I never saw anyone but Dad who would even try this. It could only work with Dad's no-chase no-twirl style of roping. If you chased after a bunch of yearlings twirling a rope, on foot or on horseback, you would drive them through the fence. Dad's style set off no stampede, and often it was a more efficient way of doing the job than working cattle in a chute.

Dad was not a cattle lover. They were his business, not his pets. He had no regrets about selling them, as long as they brought a good price. As a species, he believed them to be dumb, lazy, and contrary. He had no illusions about their innate goodness.

In the early years he kept a dairy cow or two and milked them by hand. When he thought one was swatting him in the face with her tail maliciously, he would beat her with whatever was available, usually the milking stool. I also saw him poke cows with a pitchfork. He could be equally merciless with a nurse cow that would not allow an orphaned calf to suck after being given a decent interval to accept the idea of mothering a calf not her own.

If a cow failed to produce a calf one year he sent her off to slaughter with no second chance and no sympathy. To be attractive to buyers, a bull calf had to have the right conformation and markings—straight legs and back, long deep body, attractive head, not too much red on the neck and not too much white on the back. If a calf lacked any one of the essential characteristics, Dad castrated it, no matter how outstanding it was in other respects.

If an old cow insisted on using her horns too aggressively against other cows, he might saw them off—a bloody process that must have been excruciating to the cow, to say nothing of the psychological trauma of suddenly being stripped of crown and weapons.

At the same time, he admired cattle when they showed good sense. He respected cows that produced good calves year after year, and appreciated good dispositions. He treated his herd bulls like old friends. He could walk up to them in corral or pasture, and he would always spend a few minutes scratching them behind the ears and on the brisket, patting their ribs and rumps, and rubbing their back muscles until they bowed their backs in pleasure. It was a remarkable thing to watch: a ponderous two-thousand-pound bull, majestic as an elk, turning his head to watch Dad walk away, contentment obvious in his four-square stance and affection in his eye.

My mother was not a cattle person by either upbringing or inclination, but she was not just a cattleman's wife either. She could and would feed cattle when Dad was away, break ice on the tanks, open gates, help herd cattle into a corral, and stand her ground when an angry bull bluffed a charge.

She didn't object to having a calf in her kitchen. Dad was pretty good at judging when a cow was ready to calve, and normally he would have the cow close to the buildings when she did. But occasionally a calf would be born early and Dad would find it out in the snow half-frozen. Mother would make a bed for it in the kitchen near the stove, and it would stay there a few hours until it got dried off and warmed up.

And of course, whipping up a dinner for some visiting cattle buyers on a few minutes' notice was de rigueur. The Nebraska Hereford Association honored Mother and Dad jointly as "Hereford Man of the Year" in 1988, two years before Mother died. The nomenclature was awkward, but the idea was right.

Dad's knowledge of cattle accumulated over a lifetime. He grew up around them on his parents' farm near Loup City, a hundred miles northeast of Union. His job as a boy was to look after the cattle. In the morning before school he drove the milk cows to a pasture in the Loup River bottom a mile away, and in the afternoon he brought them back.

He did this on foot, which probably had a lot to do with his understanding of cattle. On a horse you don't have to outsmart the cow; you're bigger and faster and the cow will get tired before you do. On foot the opposite is true, especially if you're a young boy. The cow can outrun you or, if she has a mind to, run over you. If she gets away, the rest of the herd will scatter or get in a farmer's wheat field while you're getting her back. Working cattle on foot tends to make you a careful student of the bovine mind.

Dad's parents raised Shorthorn cattle, a breed that was supposed to produce both beef and milk. It wasn't an entirely successful compromise. They were less efficient producers of beef than Herefords or Angus, and their milk was not as copious as a Holstein's and not as rich as a Jersey's or Guernsey's. So when Dad went into the cattle business himself, he turned his back on Shorthorns. In 1934, when he was twenty-one years old, he bought seven Hereford yearlings, and for the next fifty years he never owned any other breed, except for a few milk cows.

He chose Herefords the first time just because they looked nice, but he soon became a Hereford booster. One reason he preferred them was because they were hardy enough to make it through the winter out in the open, feeding on cornstalks and a little alfalfa hay. But their principal advantage, in his eyes, was their "natural fleshing quality." This means about the same thing as "easy keeper" means in the case of a horse (or "tends to obesity" means in the case of a human): they gain weight on less feed.

The first Herefords Dad owned were ordinary "commercial" cattle but he soon switched to registered Herefords, and the purebred business suited him perfectly. For one thing, it provided an excuse—better yet, a necessity—for lavishing the kind of attention on cattle that Dad liked to give but otherwise would have considered an unjustifiable indulgence. Purebred animals require hands-on, individual attention, beginning at birth. The date of each calf's birth must be recorded, and a unique identifying number must be tattooed in the ear. It's easiest to do this in the first hours of the calf's life, when it's obvious which cow is the mother and the calf is too wobbly to run away. That's also when the cow is most protective of her offspring, however, and she often takes umbrage at the person tampering with her baby. Dad was always careful to keep the calf between him and the cow; the cow's angry eyes might be only a foot away, but with the calf between them, she wouldn't charge Dad. To produce the nicely rounded horns that registered Herefords are expected to carry, Dad put cast-iron weights on the horns of yearlings, changed the weights as necessary to get just the right shape, replaced lost weights, and removed them at precisely the right time.

The purebred business suited him for another reason: it enabled him to use talents that raising commercial cattle wouldn't have required. Raising purebreds required him to know bloodlines, predict which bull would produce the best calf with each cow, keep close watch during breeding season lest the wrong bull breed a cow. He enjoyed the meticulous record-keeping it entailed. Some of the records were needed to meet the registration requirements of the American Hereford Association, but much of it just satisfied his own impulse to keep track of things.

He kept neat ledger books recording the offspring of each cow, the breeding history of each bull, weights of young bulls and heifers at weaning and at various stages thereafter, prices of each animal bought or sold, names and addresses of buyers and sellers. He kept records of amounts of feed bought, dates cattle were put into and out of various pastures, trucking and veterinary expenses, and deaths. We had a tall fake-mahogany secretary-bookcase with a slant-front that folded down for writing, and almost every night Dad sat there, recording things in his tally books.

He liked the social, professional, and organizational dimensions of the business—the tours, shows, and auctions put on by the local, regional, and national Hereford associations. Even more, he liked the company of Hereford breeders, who all knew (or at least knew of) each other. In what was otherwise a solitary way of life, belonging to that fraternity offered special satisfaction.

Most of all, he enjoyed the challenges of organizing, promoting, and conducting his own auctions. From the late 1940s to the 1960s, he had at least one sale every winter, sometimes two, at which he auctioned the year's production of young bulls and heifers. Well in advance, he chose a primary date and an alternate "blizzard date." He took the photos of the featured bulls, composed the copy for the sale catalog, designed a "sale bill"—a poster announcing the auction—and negotiated a contract with a printer.

He addressed the catalogs to past and prospective buyers by hand, and traveled western Nebraska and the near edges of Kansas and Colorado, posting the sale bills in windows of feed stores, cafes, sale barns, implement dealers, and grocery stores.

He booked an auctioneer, recruited ring men, and arranged for a ladies' group to serve lunch. He liked to hold the sale at home, and he owned various ranches over the years, so several times he built complete sale facilities—bleacher seats made of straw bales, a sale ring, auctioneer's stand, and pens.

On the day of the sale he was host, producer, director, and publicist of the show, and most of the year's income was dependent on its success. Dad's cattle auctions were the events of his life that most fully used his many talents.

Dad's success in the Hereford business eventually separated us slightly from the Union community. Everyone else raised commercial cattle, which they bought and sold locally. In the early years we sold many of our cattle to our neighbors. Breeding their commercial cows to registered bulls they bought from us didn't give them registered cattle, but it helped them produce bigger and better calves. As the quality and reputation of our cattle increased, they began to find buyers farther afield—registered Hereford breeders from the Sandhills and elsewhere who wanted to add our bloodlines to their herds.

When strangers began asking the neighbors for directions to our place, it set us apart. Just as the Tetros were different because of their town friends, we were different because we had callers and business dealings that our neighbors didn't. I don't think that was resented, but it did mean we weren't as fully dependent on the community as others were.

Dad died at age ninety-four. In his last ten or fifteen years, he turned his back on the cattle business—quit reading *The Hereford Journal,* quit visiting his friends among the Hereford breeders, and quit following the business. He was fond of the memories, but not nostalgic. He voiced doubt as to whether all the time he had lavished on his cattle was justified.

I don't know whether Dad ever admitted to himself that he was in the registered Hereford business because it gave him pleasure. He was a severely practical man. It was not in his nature to trade dollars for pleasure. After he retired he became an avid collector of old tools, advertising knives, and safety razors. He loved showing them off and he traded safety razors with collectors all over the world. But his greatest satisfaction was in buying cheap and selling dear. When he showed off his acquisitions, he always told how much he had paid and how much the piece was worth. Paying more than a piece was worth just because he coveted it would have been unthinkable.

While he was in the cattle business, he would not have consciously foregone income for the pleasure of raising registered cattle. But in later years he could not ignore what his meticulous records told him: that he didn't make much more money on his registered Herefords than he would have made on commercial cattle. He also realized that the modest fortune he accumulated had more to do with his success in buying and selling land than it did with profits from the Hereford business.

He was seventy-five when the Nebraska Hereford Association named him "Hereford Man of the Year." By this time he had lived in Missouri many years and no longer owned any Herefords. My sisters Elaine and Ellen say he was inordinately puffed up at the award banquet, embarrassing our mother by his lack of modesty. I wasn't there and didn't see him until a month or so later. By then he seemed curiously indifferent to the award. Maybe by then his usual clear-eyed realism had kicked in and he realized he had taken the honor too seriously. Upon reflection, he no doubt recognized that organizations have a finite supply of potential honorees and are as likely to reward longevity and conformity as real achievement. The award had come too late to have any commercial value as an endorsement of his breeding program. The uneasy suspicion that raising registered Herefords was an indulgence had probably returned. Like all gods, Mammon torments his followers when they stray.

After the horse accident that crushed his leg in 1967, Dad went on raising cattle for a few more years, hobbling on one bad leg and another that was quickly going bad from compensating for its mate. Then he gradually eased out of the business by turning his Herefords over to others to care for in exchange for a share of the profits. Eventually he sold out altogether.

I have many fond memories of my father working cattle, but one of the dearest is of him limping around the corral during his last years as an active cattleman, teaching my sons, aged eight and ten, to rope calves his special way.

*"I had three younger sisters, all within
six years of my age, but Nancy is the
only one who figured as an actor in
my world." Above: the Anderson
children, circa 1950. From left, Ellen,
Elaine, Nancy and me.*

[16]

Women

I GREW UP IN A VERY MALE WORLD. My father is everywhere in my recollections, doing things I wanted to do, being the person I aspired to be. My mother appears only now and then, always in a supporting role, even though she was a strong-willed woman who in another time and place would have lived her own life. I had three younger sisters, all within six years of my age, but Nancy is the only one who figured as an actor in my world. She was a tomboy, a calf rider and football player, tough and brave. Elaine and Ellen appear in my childhood memories only as part of the background. Ellen has a memory that pretty well captures our relationship: the four of us are walking single-file along the gravel road to school. I'm at the front, ignoring my sisters except to occasionally bark at them to keep up.

To some extent, the blanks in my memory are products of the culture I grew up in. The women in our world were defined by their relationship to men—they were wives, widows, mothers, girlfriends, and old maids. The schoolteacher was the only woman who held a job, and even that was a secondary identity: the teacher was a young woman in search of a husband, an older woman whose services were no longer needed full-time at home, or an old maid or widow.

Not being paired up was a malady to be cured if possible and pitied if not. A single man of any age was teased endlessly about getting married. Singleness of females was a joking matter only up until a certain age; after that, it was a subject to be discreetly unmentioned, like an unfortunate disease. That age came early; by seventeen a girl was expected to have her mind on marriage, and if she hadn't succeeded by her mid-twenties her lack of a mate would enter the unmentionable phase.

It was a culture in which all roles were sex-specific, but I embraced its maleness with undue enthusiasm. By the time I was seven or eight, I paid attention to girls only as girlfriends. I grew up incapable of thinking of a person's sex as secondary—unable to see females as playmates or classmates or colleagues or leaders first and women second. I've spent most of my life trying to outgrow that blinkered view of women.

My brother Walt is eleven years younger than I. He never attended country school because we moved away from Union when he was less than two years old. I left home when he was seven, so the day-to-day influences in his formative years were our three sisters, six to nine years older than him. Walt and I are close, as close as brothers separated by eleven years and three sisters can be, and we're both very much our father's sons. But he shows more of our mother's influence, and it is obvious he grew up better prepared than I for life in a world that at least aspires to equality of the sexes.

I'm sure the male dominance was a disaster for at least some of the girls I grew up with. It no doubt discouraged some from pursuing lives that didn't follow the prescribed route, coerced some into marriages of desperation, and denied many the exhilaration of open-ended possibilities.

It's not that girls were explicitly coerced or denied. My parents never forbade Nancy's tomboy escapades, and I don't think they ever tried to push any of my sisters into prescribed female roles. But my sisters, like other girls, were living in a man's world.

Sexist as we were, we weren't misogynist. Jokes about lady drivers were staples in radio comedy and newspaper comics at the time, but jokes about henpecked husbands seemed more apt to us. Our instinct wasn't to deprecate women but to elevate them, to exaggerate their influence rather than minimize it. A neighbor's decision to go to town on Saturday instead of finishing the planting would most likely be ascribed to his wife's influence, and his decision to stay and plant instead of going to town might also be ascribed to her. If you asked a rancher if he planned to buy a new bull, he might say, "If the missus will let me."

The wife of one of our neighbors became pregnant some years

after they had had their first son and daughter. She took to bed and didn't get up until the baby was born. Her husband was a busy farmer but he also kept house, cooked, and took care of the children and the bedridden wife until the baby came. It was widely assumed that the wife's indisposition had more to do with revenge for an unwanted pregnancy than medical necessity. Some men made fun of the husband for letting her get away with it, but people were more bemused by her spunk than offended by her audacity. She was welcomed back into the life of the community after the baby was born.

Most of us weren't more than a generation or two from the Old Country (usually Germany or Scandinavia), where country women were field hands. Many of the women in our community could drive a tractor or milk a cow in an emergency, but any man whose wife did man's work regularly was considered old-fashioned, or worse, "odd."

The only organized activity exclusively for women was the Ladies' Aid Society, and even that reinforced the role of women as helpmates. When a farmer was in the hospital and the neighbors came en masse to harvest his crop, Ladies' Aid served lunch. When a wife was sick or had a baby, Ladies' Aid was there with meals for the family and somebody to look after the children.

During World War II, Ladies' Aid took cakes and roasting ears to the Canteen at North Platte. Trains carrying servicemen to or from the war stopped in North Platte to take on water. Volunteers from North Platte and all the surrounding communities organized an operation that served home-cooked food and small-town hospitality to soldiers and sailors who dashed into the depot for a few minutes during the stop. The North Platte Canteen, now famous because of Bob Greene's book *Once Upon a Town,* served six million GIs by the end of the war.

I suspect that Ladies' Aid also served the inner needs of women. It must have offered female companionship in a place where most social life was male-instigated or children-centered. It would have given its members the chance to talk woman to woman, out of the hearing of husbands and children. The elections, finances, committees, reports, and projects of Ladies' Aid probably gave women a welcome outlet for organizational and leadership skills that weren't valued elsewhere. But as I've confessed, I was pretty much oblivious to women, so I'm not about to claim that I know how women felt about Ladies' Aid or anything else.

I can't even claim to know how my mother felt about her life. She was one of thirteen children, eleven of them girls. They grew up in a four-room sod house far back in the hills. My mother was the first of her family to graduate from high school. She attended Kearney State Teachers College one summer, and she taught for a few years in one-room country schools, but she always bore the stamp of the hills, a slight awkwardness physically and socially. My father once told me that when he brought her home to meet his family for the first time, his brother Carl took him aside and told him that he shouldn't marry her because "she's a hillbilly."

The older sisters in Mother's family had helped raise the younger ones, and they remained close all their lives. Most of them lived nearby, and they liked to get together often. In the early years, Dad hated their gatherings. Their indiscriminate chattering triggered his Nordic disapproval of excessive talk. Some of them still lived to the tempo of the hills, and their inability to arrive within an hour or two of the appointed time irritated him inordinately. Mother was fiercely loyal to her family, and her attempts to defend them against Dad's criticism often led to bitter arguments. Dad's disdain for her family must have pained Mother deeply, and the fact that it also infected me must have compounded her grief.

I now realize that much of the strain between my father and my mother's family was inherited. Dad's family was quintessentially Northern European. His parents had both emigrated from Sweden as young people. His people embraced Scandinavian notions of correctness in deportment and personal style. His father came from peasant stock, but his mother's family had been prosperous landowners in Sweden until a bankruptcy in the 1880s plunged the family into poverty. His mother and her sister came to America as penniless immigrants, but they were educated and had been reared in comfortable circumstances, and they retained an old-world social consciousness. Although neither of them attained wealth or social position in America, they both counted among their friends a few of the prominent ladies in their communities, a fact that made my father proud.

Mother always said her heritage was "Scotch, Irish, English, and Dutch," but I think it was mainly Irish and English by way of Appalachia. (Her grandparents' names were Bailey, Porter, Greene, and Conley.) They came to Nebraska from Kentucky in covered wagons and homesteaded in Custer County, a part of the state more hospitable to outlaws and rattlesnakes than settlers. Mother's father played the fiddle and hosted barn dances in their remote rural community, called Pleasant Hill.

Mother and her family were jovial and fatalistic. They laughed extravagantly, as if laughter itself could make things better. I inherited my mother's taste for corny humor and her tendency to laugh too easily—like her, I thought Minnie Pearl was a terrific comedienne and *Hee-Haw* was a hilarious television show. Life dealt Mother's family few material rewards and many illnesses, losses, and disappointments, but their laughter and unconditional familial love rarely wavered. They were religious, tending toward the fundamentalist creeds, but not judgmental.

There were no social pretensions in my mother's family. They were egalitarian, perhaps to a fault. They seemed to really believe that we're all God's children and that every life is equally valuable, or at least redeemable. Judging character and assigning blame didn't interest them. Mother was loved and respected by her family and our neighbors, and social acceptance beyond those circles didn't matter to her, except perhaps to please my father. Mother never tried very hard to acquire the graces that her upbringing hadn't provided, perhaps because that would have distanced her from her beloved sisters. There was enough of the social climber in both my father and me to make Mother's willful ordinariness an irritant. We were embarrassed when she went around the house with her hose rolled down around her ankles, or laughed too long at her own weak joke.

After Mother's death, Dad and I both came to realize that our attitudes toward Mother's family were cruel to Mother and unfair to her family. We had allowed our own predilections to blind us; we failed to see that Mother's people embraced an admirable set of values and were unshakably faithful to them. Sadly, our eyes opened too late to give Mother any comfort.

To all appearances, Mother relished her life as wife and mother. She was the dominant voice in how we were raised. She made sure our chores didn't make us late for school and enrolled us in summer Bible school even if our help was needed at home. She insisted that we have piano lessons and new clothes and family photos when Dad might have thought it better to spend the money on cattle or land.

The neighbors loved her. She was a fixture in Ladies' Aid, always there with a covered dish for someone who was ill, ever ready to keep a neighbor's children. She was indiscriminately supportive. Dad was judgmental and demanding; Mother was forgiving to a fault. She found everyone interesting and worthy. I don't think I ever heard her criticize anyone. She was greatly offended by the things Richard Nixon had done, but when he resigned the presidency she only felt sorry for him: "What in the world could have made him do those things? He was such an able man, and had accomplished so much. It's just such a shame."

She became the family historian, not only for her family but also for Dad's, and later for each of her own children's families. She kept track of birthdays and anniversaries, sent wedding gifts and sympathy notes and Christmas cards to an ever-expanding universe of family and friends, compiled genealogies, and wrote family entries for local community histories.

For all her apparent contentment, however, Mother seemed to harbor an undercurrent of dissatisfaction, particularly in her later years. It was not in her nature to complain, but occasionally some passing comment would betray a wistfulness about things that might have been. Sometimes she would wonder if, instead of getting married, she should have gone to California as some of her sisters had done. Late in life she allowed herself to wonder out loud if things might have been better for us kids if she and Dad had divorced. I think the question was hypothetical, unloosed by the new acceptability of divorce. When we kids were little, the unacceptability of divorce and Mother's subordination of self to family wouldn't have allowed her to even think about it.

I've always called my father "Dad," but sometime in adolescence I started saying "Mother" rather than "Mom." I see now that I was deliberately distancing myself from her, denying the intimacy that "Mom" implies. That surely hurt her, but she never withdrew her love from me.

In what turned out to be her last days, I was visiting for Christmas. Suffering from lymph edema, she was unable to tie her shoes. I knelt and tied them for her, and then looked up and saw her smiling down at me beatifically, lost in the unquestioning, unwavering love that was her hallmark. Later that day as I left to fly home, she hugged me and whispered, "I love you, Son. Goodbye." Two days later she died.

My conversations with her were always within the conventions of the parent-child relationship. After her death, I occasionally managed to escape those prescribed roles in conversations with my father, but Mother died before I understood how important it is for parents and children to know each other as people.

"I knew my paternal grandparents
only when they were both quite old.
We visited them several times a
year at Loup City, a two-hour drive
from Union." Above: Grandma and
Grandpa Anderson, circa 1946.

[17]

The Old Swedes

FOR MY FIFTH BIRTHDAY, my Grandfather Anderson gave me a
hatchet. I doubt that it was new; he was a frugal old Swede who
wouldn't have wasted money on a new one if a good used one could be
had. He was also a proud man, so he didn't give me a dull hatchet; he
believed a man should always keep his tools sharp. He probably spent
a pleasant hour sharpening it, straddling the rusty seat on the old foot-
operated grindstone that sat outside the tumble-down workshop on
his farm, pushing the tool to and fro to keep it in contact with the badly
out-of-round stone. When he gave it to me, it had a good keen edge.

When I got home, I happily put the hatchet to use making miniature corrals. I used it to split off "posts" from some left-over cedar
roofing shingles, used the flat side of the hatchet to drive the narrow
ends in the ground, and strung grocery twine from post to post to make
the "barbed wire." When the shingles were five or six inches wide,
splitting off half-inch wide strips was easy enough, but when there was
only an inch or two left, it became more of an adventure.

Eventually a finger got too close. I sliced my left index finger
diagonally from the outermost joint about two-thirds of the way
through the nail. Only the nail and a little piece of flesh kept the end
attached to the rest of the finger.

For the next forty years, my mother loved to tell how I came running into the house, blood dripping on the floor, yelling, "Mommy!
Mommy! I've killed myself." We had to go to town and get Doc Pyle to
stitch it up.

Grandpa wasn't at all contrite about having given me the means
to hurt myself. He just hoped I had learned a lesson. The lesson, of

course, was not that I shouldn't play with dangerous things; it was that I should keep my fingers out of the way.

Grandpa Anderson had seventeen grandchildren. I'm sure he loved us all, but the evidence of that was not easily recognizable. His standard greeting for kids was painful. As if he were thumping a watermelon, he rapped us on the head with a huge, rock-hard knuckle. "Let's see if there's anything in there," he'd say. Some of my female cousins say this ritual made them dread going to visit our grandparents.

For boys, he had another token of affection. When a grandson came within range, he would grab him in a headlock and briskly rub his knuckles into the boy's scalp. He called that a "Dutch rub." When Grandpa's Dutch rub no longer made you cry, it was a sign you were growing up.

A year or two after he gave me the hatchet, he gave me and my cousin Roger a tool chest each. He hired a carpenter to make them from the rosewood of an old piano Grandpa had bought as junk. They were the size of a large suitcase, with a space in the bottom for planes, hammers, and other large tools, a removable tray for smaller tools, and holders in the top for three large hand saws.

Grandpa made fun of me for being barely able to lift the chest even without anything in it, but I know he gave it as sign of confidence that I would one day be a man substantial enough to need a good tool chest.

It would have been difficult for him to imagine a world in which a tool chest would be of no use to a man. In Sweden, his father, Anders, was a tenant farmer who was locally famous for his strength. Anders's nickname was Lonken—strongman—and to this day there is a bronze marker at the edge of a field in Dalsland, marking the location of "Lonke-torpet," the farm where Lonken lived, near Jarbo.

Anders came to the U.S. around 1880 to join an uncle who had homesteaded in the Loup River country of Nebraska while the Sioux still considered it their territory. He somehow accumulated enough money to buy a package deal for his wife, Kajsa, and their six children in 1882: second class on a steamer from Göteborg to Hull; after customhouse examination there, on to Liverpool; then across the Atlantic in steerage aboard a Royal Mail steamer to New York, thence by train (second class), to Grand Island, Nebraska—all for 835 kroner. My grandfather, Carl, was thirteen. On the crossing two of his younger brothers fell ill. They died shortly after arrival.

Anders and Kajsa homesteaded in the hills a few miles from Loup City. I don't know whether my grandfather ever attended school. I'm not even sure he could read or write; I don't recall ever seeing any evidence that he could. I suspect he spent his youth in back-breaking labor on the farm, living up to the legacy of Lonken.

My grandmother's family had been prosperous land-owning far-mers in Sweden for many generations, until they were bankrupted in the economic collapse that struck Sweden in 1880s. Her father, Sven Erickson, had co-signed a note for someone, the debtor defaulted, and the creditor demanded payment from my great-grandfather. The bankruptcy broke up the family and left them all destitute. Two of the sons emigrated to Oslo. My grandmother, Elisabeth, eighteen years old, and her sister Mina, sixteen, emigrated to the United States. They headed for Nebraska because the only people they knew in America were Kajsa and Anders—Kajsa was their aunt.

According to family legend, the two girls were threatened with three weeks' quarantine at Ellis Island, but Elisabeth showed their rail tickets to Nebraska and the authorities, assured that the girls would be far from New York by the time they came down with smallpox, let them go.

On the long train ride from New York to Nebraska, the train stopped periodically and at some stops an announcement was made that passengers would have time to get off and buy food. But Elisabeth and Mina, who spoke no English, couldn't understand the announce-ments and feared that if they got off they would be left behind. Even-tually Mina's hunger overcame her fear and she dashed off the train. For the rest of her life, Elisabeth described those few minutes, when she feared she would never see her sister again, as the worst time of the trip. But Mina got back with a couple of loaves of bread. The girls clung to each other, then cried and laughed and ate.

In Nebraska, Elisabeth and Mina got work as household help and learned English. Mina changed her name to Minnie, or perhaps an employer Anglicized it for her. They had promised their parents they would return after two years, but they never did, and they never saw their family again.

After she had been in the country four years, Elisabeth married Carl—her first cousin. The family has always treated that as unremarkable, but it's perplexing to me. Loup City was mostly Swedish, so surely there were plenty of suitable nonfamily mates. No doubt they both spent most of their waking hours working and had few social events except family gatherings, but Minnie managed to meet and marry a German immigrant, Fred Rein. Elisabeth was twenty-two and Carl twenty-seven. Elisabeth was deeply religious and must have attended church, and one would assume that Carl had been off the farm enough times to meet some young women. They were both good-looking and would seem to have been highly eligible marriage prospects.

In any event, it seems to have been a proper courtship and marriage. They announced their engagement well in advance. Elisabeth made her wedding dress. She tried, through exchanges of letters that took six weeks each way, to arrange for her parents to come to America for the wedding. Both sets of parents seem to have been pleased with the match.

I knew my paternal grandparents only when they were both quite old. We visited them several times a year at Loup City, a two-hour drive from Union. Grandpa Anderson looked very Swedish. He was tall, blue-eyed, square-jawed, and gruff. He had a thick mustache, white like his hair but yellow at the bottom edge from drinking his coffee from a saucer. Grandma didn't look Swedish at all. She was tiny and dark skinned, with sad dark eyes. She no doubt carried the genes of the Tartars or some other race conquered and carried back to Scandinavia by the Vikings.

By the time I knew Grandma Anderson, she was stooped, shriveled, and toothless. She was as energetic and expressive as Grandpa was stolid and taciturn. He was areligious; she devoutly believed that everything is in the hands of the Lord. I never saw my grandfather display affection toward her. That doesn't prove a lot, because people of their generation abhorred public displays of affection, but I suspect my grandfather was a difficult man to love. My father respected his father, but he adored his mother, and we visited Grandma far more often in the ten years she was a widow than when they were both living.

At my grandfather's funeral, we sang "The Old Rugged Cross." I thought "The Rugged Old Cuss" would have been more fitting.

In 4-H, Nancy and I raised
breeding heifers—pretty females
who were destined to spend their
lives raising a calf every year.

[18]

The Sex Business

I DON'T REMEMBER EVER NOT KNOWING ABOUT SEX. When you grow up around livestock, you're surrounded by sex. Raising any kind of livestock is a sex-for-profit business. Raising purebred livestock is a tightly controlled sex-for-profit business. Like thoroughbred horses, each registered Hereford has a pedigree that goes back many generations. If a deviant characteristic shows up in an offspring, it casts suspicion on your diligence as a chaperone, or worse, impugns the integrity of the whole bloodline. That's why, if a trespassing bull gets in a pasture with his cows, a conscientious breeder doesn't register the calves that are born forty weeks later.

Controlling the sex lives of cattle was the essence of our business. You want your animals to procreate, but only with the mates you choose, and at times that suit your needs, not theirs. Imagine trying to achieve this with humans, who might at least know what you want and why, and you can begin to see why it's so hard with animals.

A child who grows up around this business learns many useful lessons about sex. You learn, for example, that youthful lust needs to be suppressed for a while. Young bulls and heifers are capable of reproducing by the time they're a year old, and the desire arrives as soon as the ability.

The females handle this with some poise. They're at their prettiest at this age and they carry themselves with a demure elegance that seems to say, "I'm beautiful and everybody admires me and I know it." They're capable of enticing an incautious male into a disastrous liaison, but for the most part they seem content to revel in an interlude of ripe but innocent femininity. Perhaps somewhere along its evolutionary journey the psyche of the female bovine absorbed the intuition that once she surrenders, what lies ahead is a lifetime of rapacious males, hungry babies, sad partings with adolescent offspring, and never enough rest.

The young bulls exhibit no poise at all. They quarrel incessantly, sometimes over real issues such as feed and water, but often over silly things—one thinks another is standing too close, or perceives a taunt in the other's body language. At first the fights are harmless; they bluff and posture, try out fighting stances, push and shove a bit, and then walk away. But as they get older the quarrels fester and the testosterone grows more relentless. They begin fighting for keeps, long exhausting fights that can go on, intermittently, for days.

Now the breeder's experience and judgment are called upon. The bulls need to learn to fight. Holding the affections of a harem of fifty cows requires a certain amount of swagger, and the youthful fighting is where bulls acquire that machismo. A bull also needs to learn the art of self-defense. Many of our bull buyers were ranchers who raised commercial cattle. Those ranchers don't care which bull breeds which cows, so they run their cattle in large herds with several bulls. If a bull is to do his part in a commercial herd, he has to be able to keep the other bulls from seducing his cows.

Even if the bull is destined for a less competitive life in a registered herd where he will have his own exclusive set of concubines, there will be times in his life when he has to fight. Eventually a neighboring bull will develop an irresistible attraction for one of his cows. The interloper may wander into his transgression fortuitously, as when a big rain washes out the fence, or he may create his own opportunity by knocking down the fence. (These possibilities call to mind the Waylon Jennings line, "The devil made me do it the first time, the second time I done it on my own.") The interloper is more interested in loving than fighting, but the ancient possessive instincts of the bull who is about to be cuckolded will compel him to defend his monopoly—even if he would be glad, in his heart of hearts, to let the interloper have what he wants.

So we allowed our young bulls to fight, to a point. But they can hurt each other or themselves—break a horn, sprain a foot, or injure a back. And even if they don't, constant fighting erodes their physical condition. The trick is to let them scrimmage until they are competent fighters, then separate them.

The reason the lust of pubescent heifers and bulls has to be suppressed is that early sex isn't good for them. If a heifer breeds as soon as she can, energy and nutrients that her own body needs are diverted to the gestating calf, and the heifer never grows quite as rangy as she could have. Also, two-year-old heifers have a lot of trouble giving birth. Our goal was to produce big calves, and we chose bulls with that goal in mind, but big calves from not-quite-full-grown mothers is a recipe for trouble.

Early sex can stunt the growth of young bulls too, but with them the matter is a bit more complicated. Occasional one-night stands probably wouldn't hurt them, but that wouldn't advance our goals. In our view the purpose of sex was procreation, and not on an occasional basis. Breeding one bull to one cow and another to the next would be an inefficient use of our time and the bull's capacities. A bull is expensive, he is capable of breeding a lot of cows, and when he does so you get a nice uniform crop of half-sisters and -brothers. So we weren't interested in letting young bulls exploit their virility until they were ready to do it wholesale. Barring an exhilarating accident like a gate left open, young bulls never got a chance to sample a little experimental adolescent sex.

The reason the bull's sexual plunge has to be delayed is that he dives in too enthusiastically. Breeding cows is hard work. Part of it is the act itself, which requires considerable athleticism from a bull that weighs fifteen hundred to two thousand pounds. Strained backs and sprained ankles are common ailments.

The preliminaries are also exhausting. Cattle don't indulge in sex for fun. They breed only when the cow is ready to get pregnant. The bull therefore has to do a considerable amount of socializing in order to find a receptive female. Cows hang out together, feigning indifference. They demand that the male seek them out, so the bull has to go where the ladies congregate, and mingle.

This ritual has evolved more efficiently in their species than in ours; a certain smell in the female's urine is a sure signal that she craves his body. But first the cow wants to be pursued for a while, perhaps so her friends will see that the only male around has chosen *her*. So she walks away, obliging the bull to show his devotion by following her wherever her whim takes them. Some cows like a secluded little hide-away, even if it takes a long hike and a lot of hill-climbing to get there. Some are brazen enough to Do It right in front of the crowd.

Sex consumes a lot of time and energy in exchange for its mo-mentary ecstasy. A mature bull in top condition can breed forty to fifty cows in a three-month season. A two-year-old should be limited to half that many, and cautiously at that. My father had a little speech he gave to any inexperienced breeder who bought one of his young bulls:

"An old bull, you don't have to worry too much about him. You can turn him in with a bunch of cows and he'll pace himself. He'll service one cow and then he'll go lay in the shade the rest of the day. A young bull, he don't have sense enough to do that. He breeds one cow and right away he's off chasing another one. In a week or two he'll be worn out."

The preventive is to turn the young bull in with the cows for a few days, take him out for a few days' rest, and continue this until the bull learns the sweetness of satisfaction postponed. Despite Dad's careful advice, several times buyers brought back worn-out young bulls, claiming they were impotent. Dad always gave them their money back, but usually it was obvious the bull had ceased to breed because he was too debilitated to do so. Sometimes we were able to nurture them back to healthy breeding condition, but occasionally the damage was permanent.

Enforcing abstinence in adolescent males and females is not an easy thing to do. Putting young bulls and heifers in adjoining pastures would be disastrous, of course, as foolish as assigning unchaperoned teenaged girls and boys to adjoining rooms. A fence is no match for lust, as the experience of all species demonstrates: randy dogs dig under them, and wayward humans jump them even when they are made of law and religion. Cattle knock them down. In range country the standard fence is three or four strands of barbed wire, which suffices against all the lesser temptations, even greener grass on the other side. But if it's heifers on the other side, a barbed wire fence is no obstacle to a bull.

This is as true of old bulls as young ones. For that reason, you can't even put heifers in a pasture adjoining a cow herd. An old bull may be worn to a frazzle by his domestic obligations with his mature mates, but if he sees a comely heifer next door he will discover reserves of lust he didn't know he had. You can put each of two old bulls with a herd of mature cows in adjoining pastures, and the fence usually will hold them to their respective conjugal obligations. But if there are heifers next door, an old bull will be through the fence as quickly as his sons and grandsons.

Occasionally a cattleman overestimates his power. He builds a fence the cattle can't knock down and then puts temptation on the other side. This usually fails, but only after inflicting tragic consequences. Love finds a way, and the way is usually through the fence. Many bulls have been ruined this way, their penises cut to shreds by the barbed wire.

Celibacy can be enforced only by keeping temptation away. Our places were divided by many fences, so we could put young bulls or heifers in isolated pastures. The ideal is a pasture bordered by a road on one side (so you can drive by frequently to look for signs of hanky-panky) and fields or unoccupied pastures on the other sides. Unfortunately there are never enough of those, so the next best solution is to double-fence. Instead of one fence between pastures, you build two, at least ten yards apart. This creates a no-sniff zone, which prevents the kind of through-the-fence affairs that inflict the damage described above.

Even so, when love is in the air it communicates across the chasm, and you will often see well-worn paths along both outsides of a double fence, where thwarted lovers have paced back and forth for days, foolishly believing the bromide that where there's a will there's a way.

When I was about ten, my friend Joe Tetro and I came up with a dastardly idea for a practical joke. Although fate squelched our prank, the plan shows that we knew our schoolmates understood animal anatomy as well as we did.

Joe had ordered a taxidermy kit from the back of a magazine. He told the teacher about it, and she was eager to have him try it out and bring a preserved specimen to school. Joe studied the manual that came with the kit, which assured him that with careful study and practice he could stuff birds and rabbits and snakes, but also advised him to be on the lookout for natural materials that, if properly treated and preserved, could be made into useful everyday items such as belts and purses.

In faithful obedience to this advice, Joe hit upon just the right material to make a quirt. A quirt is a semi-flexible whip, about two feet long and less than an inch thick, that horsemen use. Joe astutely identified a natural material just the right size and shape, with about the desired degree of flexibility: a bull's penis.

That organ has a distinctive pink-orange color, which led me to encourage Joe to carry his idea one step further: he should take the finished quirt to school and show it to the teacher. The quirt would be a useful everyday implement, just as the taxidermy kit suggested. But its origins would be obvious, even to a teacher, because in our world it was hard not to observe a bull's private parts. The kids would snicker and guffaw and the teacher would be mortified, but she wouldn't dare punish Joe because he had only done what she asked. We thought it was the perfect prank. Neither of us bore the teacher any malice. It was just a red-blooded joke, the kind our fathers would have appreciated.

All we needed was a dead bull. One of the Tetro bulls had died not long before Joe received the taxidermy kit. That event had given Joe the idea, but in the meantime that bull had been hauled off to the rendering plant. For months, we both were on the alert for bull deaths anywhere in the neighborhood. We inquired about the health of old bulls, looked for lame bulls, and prayed for some young bull to work himself to death. But all the bulls stayed healthy, and the quirt caper died for want of an organ donor, joining the long list of brilliant ideas that have been denied a place in history by the caprice of fate.

[19]

Violent Death

EARLY ON, I came to appreciate both the ordinariness and the mystery of death. When I was four my cousin Junior Dainton was dragged to death by a horse. I have no contemporaneous memory of the event, but it was part of my earliest understanding of life. The image of Junior's body bouncing along behind a running horse has been with me for as long as I can remember.

Junior was ten when it happened. The story I remembered was that he had just got new boots and was eager to play cowboy. He was learning to rope, and if he practiced the way most of us did, he would have been throwing his loop at fence posts, buckets, and chickens. For some reason he had tied one end of the rope around one of his new boots. He threw the loop at a horse, probably not contemplating the consequences if he should happen to connect. The horse naturally ran, jerking Junior off his feet and dragging him around the pasture by one leg.

Now I'm told that isn't how it happened at all. Junior's sister Marilyn, who was six at the time, recalls a very different scenario. The Daintons lived on a small ranch in Eureka Valley in Custer County, about fifty miles from where we lived. Because the mail route didn't pass by their house, their mailbox was on another road some distance away. Just before lunch on a hot August day, Junior got on his horse and rode off to get the mail. Paul, the husband and father, was helping a neighbor thresh wheat a few miles away.

When lunch was ready, Junior's mother, Wilma, called him to come in. When he didn't appear, she and Marilyn went looking for him. They immediately saw the riderless horse standing in the yard, Junior on the ground nearby. When they approached, the horse ran and they saw that Junior's foot was entangled in the reins.

Wilma got the horse stopped and untangled Junior's foot. Marilyn held the gate open while Wilma carried Junior into the house. They had no telephone so they walked a mile to a neighbor's house to call the farm where Paul was working. Because they walked rather than ran to the neighbors', and because they called for Paul rather than a doctor, I assume it must have been obvious to Wilma that Junior was already dead.

Marilyn says Junior's parents surmised that when he dismounted to open a gate, he put the reins under his foot so he could use both hands to deal with the gate. Something, maybe a snake, spooked the horse and it bolted with Junior's foot caught in the reins. The horse would have been spooked anew by Junior dragging behind, yelling, no doubt.

From the beginning, I had a hard time understanding how Junior died, and now I'm less sure than ever. Many riders have been dragged to death, but it's usually because they get a foot caught in a stirrup. It's easy for a horse to pull a man who's hanging by a stirrup. The rider gets kicked in the head or stepped on, and injuries like that are easily fatal. But a horse can't go far with the reins tied to a sixty-pound weight. On the plains where there was nothing to tie a horse to, travelers carried five- or ten-pound weights in their buggies and wagons, and with those tied to the reins and dropped on the ground, a horse or even a team wouldn't move more than a few feet. There were no rocks in that country, and few trees; nothing, really, for the victim to hit. So even if the horse runs some distance, the injuries might be gruesome but shouldn't be fatal.

When I told my father I was writing about Junior's death and asked him for details, he said, "Well, a horse drug him to death. I don't know that there's a whole lot more to say about it." In a sense he's right. No one will ever know how Junior died, and no amount of theorizing or speculating or calculating will take away the mystery of it.

I do wonder how the new boots and the rope got into the version of the story that embedded itself in my mind. Maybe I confused the real story with my father's admonitions that you should never tie a rope to yourself. Maybe the new boots were a wish that somehow became entangled with a nightmare; maybe they were a rationalization of my disappointment over never having new boots.

Wilma and Paul never fully recovered from Junior's death. It was a cloud on their faces, a sadness in their eyes, for the rest of their lives. I never heard them mention it, but I never saw them without being reminded of it.

At Maywood one of our neighbors was named Huston Anderson. He was not related to us, but he and his wife Leola became close friends of my parents, and remained so long after we moved away. Huston and his son Bob, then eighteen and about to graduate from Maywood High School, were rounding up cattle when a heifer ducked under Bob's running horse. The horse flipped and landed on top of Bob, killing him. Bob was younger than I, and I was grown when he was killed, so his death didn't shape my outlook the way Junior's did. But it was the kind of accident we all knew could happen anytime.

Tractors and machinery were murderous too. In any gathering of men—at the sale barn or a livestock show or a farm sale—there was always a fair sampling of missing arms, feet, and hands, lost in some piece of machinery.

When I was just beginning to drive a tractor, a neighbor boy was killed by one. Junior Blede was using a tractor and a ditching machine to make an irrigation ditch when the tractor overturned and pinned him beneath. I didn't know him well, but he lived only four or five miles away. We passed the site of his death every time we went to Brady, and it gave me a healthy respect for the dangers of tractors.

Another neighbor boy was killed while he was refueling the motor on an irrigation pump. Farmers at that time used siphon tubes to carry water from the laterals (small ditches) to the corn rows. If the water level dropped in the lateral they had to restart each tube by hand, so they tried to keep the pump running and the water flowing continuously. That meant the engine had to be refueled while it was running—a ridiculously dangerous procedure because the gas tank was usually located directly above the engine so the fuel could feed by gravity.

Refueling meant pouring gasoline from a five-gallon can into a funnel tucked into the mouth of the gas tank. If you poured too fast, the fuel would overflow the funnel, and if you overfilled the tank the gas would overflow onto the engine.

The boy must have spilled a little gas on the engine, because it erupted in a fireball that engulfed the pump house. Dad happened on the scene moments later and found the father frantically trying to find his son.

"I tried to tell him maybe the boy had managed to crawl out into the weeds," Dad told us when he got home, "but we both knew pretty well he was in that pump house."

My mother had twelve brothers and sisters and my father eight, so I had lots of aunts and uncles. It's a good thing, because the mortality rate among them was high.

My uncle Ed France had a cranky old tractor that was hard to start on really cold mornings. Ed got in the habit of starting a small fire on the ground under the engine to warm it up. He would build the fire and go about his chores, and when he came back half an hour later the tractor would be warmed up enough to start. The tractor was tall enough that a small fire shouldn't reach the engine, but one morning the flames reached a little too high or a little fuel leaked out. The gas tank blew up and Uncle Ed died of a heart attack.

Another uncle, Archie Hubbard, drove a road grader for the county, maintaining the gravel roads in the area around Brady. He was attempting to help someone get a car out of the ditch when the machine rolled backward and pinned him between it and the car. His pelvis was crushed. He lived a few more years but never really recovered.

My favorite uncle, Ernie Booth, had a drinking problem and eventually lost his job as foreman of the Upper 96 Ranch. There weren't many employment alternatives except the alfalfa mills that operated in all the towns up and down the valley. The mills bought alfalfa in the field from farmers, dehydrated it in huge gas-fired drums, and compressed it into pellets that were shipped by train to the feedlots of the Midwest to be fed to livestock as a protein supplement.

Ernie got a job with the mill in Brady. Because he was skilled and experienced with machinery, he was made field manager, in charge of tractors, choppers, and other equipment. One day in October, just a few months after leaving the ranch, Ernie was moving a tractor from the mill in Gothenburg to its sister mill in Brady. It would never have occurred to the mill management to haul the tractor on a trailer, because it took only about an hour to drive the thirteen miles, and an hour of a man's time cost only a dollar or two. (I often drove tractors back and forth between the valley and Maywood, which was forty miles, because even that took only half a day).

Ernie was driving the tractor along Highway 30, then one of the busiest two-lane highways in the country. He was undoubtedly going as fast as the tractor could go, which would have been no more than ten or twelve miles an hour. He couldn't drive entirely on the shoulder because it was too narrow, so he had one wheel on the shoulder and one on the pavement. The orange triangle that now identifies slow-moving vehicles hadn't yet been conceived. A sailor returning to duty on the West Coast overtook Ernie's tractor, misjudged how fast he was closing, and clipped the left rear wheel of the tractor. Ernie was thrown off and his skull was crushed.

When my father broke the news to me, he said, "The doc says it's a blessing he didn't live. His head just hit too hard. He would have been a pitiful thing."

Although Ernie's death was devastating for his family, it may in fact have been merciful for him. He was forty-nine years old and had never known any life but ranching. He had held the dream job for a man of his background—foreman of a great ranch—and lost it. He had moved his family from the big house on the ranch to a modest house in town. Once he had been responsible for everything that happened on a small empire; now he was only responsible for keeping the machines operating in a mill. The change in circumstances did not bode well for a man who was already an alcoholic. For me, and I hope for his children, Ernie's early death protected the memory of a lusty, loud, mischievous, irrepressible cowboy.

Trains were another frequent killer. The main line of the Union Pacific Railroad, which ran beside Highway 30 on the north side of the river, was a major route from Chicago to California. It was a double track, so trains going one way didn't even slow down for trains going the other direction, and there were many sidings where slow freights could pull off to let the fast freights and passenger trains pass. The diesel-powered streamliners went eighty to a hundred miles per hour and didn't slow down for most of the towns.

We had to cross the tracks to get to either Gothenburg or Brady. The main crossing in Gothenburg had flashing lights and cross-arms that came down to block traffic while a train was passing. Three other crossings at Gothenburg, the crossing at Brady, and all the rural crossings in between had no warning devices other than an X-shaped sign that said "RAILROAD CROSSING."

People were killed regularly, and the railroad had little incentive to try to prevent it. The cow-catchers on the front of the locomotives were designed to knock the vehicles aside without damage to the train. Even if the railroad negligently failed to provide warning devices, slow down for towns, or watch for vehicles on the track, it rarely had to pay damages because of the legal doctrine of contributory negligence. That rule of law, now widely discredited but prevalent at the time, protected the railroad from liability if the victim was the least bit negligent, and anyone who tried to cross in the path of a train could usually be charged with some negligence. A frequent scenario was that a motorist waited for a train on the near track to pass, then started across and was blindsided by a train coming from the other direction and shielded from view by the first train.

Train deaths often seemed inexplicable. For one thing, it's hard to understand how a person can fail to notice a train. For another, the violence of the collision often makes it difficult to reconstruct what happened. The summer after I graduated from high school I had a job working for one of the alfalfa mills. Two or three of us were working the overnight shift in a warehouse beside the railroad tracks in Gothenburg.

About three o'clock in the morning, there was a terrible scream of steel wheels scraping along steel rails, and somebody shouted that a train must have hit a car. As soon as we found a flashlight we ran down the track a couple of hundred yards to the front of the train. A mangled car was pasted to the front of the locomotive. Some others had got there ahead of us and told us that there was a woman inside, dead. We shined the flashlight in the car and saw the woman. She was leaning sideways in the seat with her head against the window sill of the passenger door. Her eyes were wide open, there was not a drop of blood in sight, and she was naked from the waist up.

We learned later that she was a young wife, mother of several children. I never found out what she was doing out at three in the morning, or why she was wearing no blouse or brassiere. One of my co-workers said maybe someone who arrived on the scene before we did removed them to check for a heartbeat. She was driving from the wrong side of the tracks, where the rougher element lived, toward the respectable side where she lived. The ghostly whiteness of her naked flesh in the harsh beam of the flashlight stuck in my memory for years.

Harry Anderson, the hired hand who was supposed to be my chaperone at the Fourth of July rodeo in Curtis, was killed by a train. Harry had known Ernie Booth since they were both young men, and he had worked for Ernie from time to time at the 96 Ranch. In later years he was just a hanger-on, an old friend Ernie and Lucille tolerated and looked after.

After Ernie was killed, Harry roomed off and on at Lucille's house. He had a small cabin of his own, but he liked the company of Lucille and her children and grandchildren, and he ate there frequently even when he wasn't a roomer. Lucille was a wonderful cook and always seemed to like having someone extra to cook for. You might think such an arrangement between a widow woman and a bachelor would set tongues wagging, but suspicion would never cross the mind of anyone who knew either Lucille or Harry, and in Brady everybody knew them both.

Harry's other hangout was the beer joint next door to Thanel's gas station. Lucille's house and the beer joint were both on the north side of the tracks and Harry's cabin was on the south side. One day a few years after Ernie's death, Harry drove a little too far to the right on the crossing and got his car stuck on the railroad tracks. He got out and went around the car to survey the problem, and while he was doing so a train came along and hit both him and the car. Harry may have been drunk, but not necessarily; he was so hard of hearing in his last years that the train might not have made itself heard over the noise of the wind and Harry cursing his bad luck.

The boy from Union School who limped to school wearing a steel brace on his polio-shriveled leg was named Stanley Anderson (no kin to either Harry Anderson or us). He became a talented musician with his own country-western band. He tried for years to make the jump from local dance band to recording artist but never succeeded, and eventually he stepped in front of a train in Brady.

The train death that affected my family most deeply was that of Leonard Berniklau, whom everyone called Bernie. Bernie came from eastern Nebraska. His parents divorced when he was thirteen or fourteen and his father got a job at Pawnee Springs Ranch, the biggest ranch in the county. It was a few miles up the valley and across the river from the Upper 96 Ranch. Pawnee Springs owned all the land for miles on both sides of the Union Pacific tracks from Maxwell to North Platte. Bernie and his father moved into the bunkhouse with the other single men.

Bernie worked on the ranch, but also went to high school in Maxwell. When his father moved on, Bernie chose to stay. The ranch manager and his wife took Bernie under their wing and made sure he finished high school. There he met my cousin, Marjorie Booth. Marj was the daughter of Ernie's brother Fred Booth. (Ernie married my father's sister and Fred married my mother's sister Mildred).

Marj was a beautiful and sexy girl, and Bernie was a handsome young man. He looked a little like the actor Gig Young. He had a brilliant smile, perfect white teeth, and dark eyes and hair. He was the kind of young man women adore: modest and polite, but also poised and self-confident. Marj and Bernie must have been the most attractive couple ever seen in Maxwell, population 300. They were married when he was twenty-one and she was sixteen.

Bernie stayed on at the ranch until the Korean War. Then he

joined the Army and was sent to Guam, where he helped build the air strip that was later used by the B-52s that bombed Vietnam. After the Korean cease-fire, he returned to the ranch and eventually became a foreman.

Pawnee Springs was so big it had two foremen, one for hay and one for cattle. Bernie was the hay foreman. In the summer the ranch hands put up hundreds of stacks of prairie hay in the wet meadows along the river, and alfalfa in fields that were a little higher and drier. In winter they hauled the hay to the Pawnee Springs cattle, which must have numbered a thousand or more.

The ranch headquarters was almost a village in its own right. There were separate houses for the manager, the two foremen, and the married hands, and the bunkhouse for the single hands. Marj and Bernie lived in the hay foreman's house and had three daughters.

Eventually the ranch management decided to make some changes. They decided to bring in a third foreman, who was to be in charge of irrigation and live in the house Marj and Bernie had occupied. Bernie could continue to work at the ranch if he wanted to, but the arrangement would not be the same. So Marj and Bernie rented a house in town and prepared to move from the ranch where Bernie had spent more than half of his forty years.

On the last morning before they were to move off the ranch, Bernie got in an International pickup to feed cattle in a pasture across the tracks. It was late November, it was foggy, and the sun was not yet up when he finished and headed back toward the ranch headquarters. The dirt road approached the tracks at a sharp angle. A highway patrolman driving on the highway beside the tracks saw the collision. He later testified that the train's headlight was out. Bernie apparently didn't see the train approaching through the fog. The train hit the pickup broadside and Bernie was killed instantly. The next day's North Platte newspaper carried a front-page photo of the mangled pickup with Bernie's body still inside.

Bernie's death was a jolt to the entire extended Bailey family. The men respected Bernie because he was upright, hard-working, and personable. The women loved him because he was handsome and charming. To be dead at forty, leaving three lovely daughters, seemed too cruel even for a clan accustomed to premature death.

There were other deaths less violent but just as brutal. My mother's older brother, Woodrow, was out in the winter air too long just after his first birthday and caught a cold. It turned into what was then called "brain fever" and he died. My grandmother's younger sister, Vera, lived nearby and had a son about the same age as Woodrow. The two families who had enjoyed their little boys together now traveled together in a buggy to Woodrow's funeral. It was bitterly cold, and on the way home Vera wrapped her baby tightly and covered his face, no doubt anxious to protect him from the fate that had befallen Woodrow. When they got home she found that the boy had suffocated. This happened long before I was born, but it was part of the family history that made death familiar to me.

My mother's younger sister Nina has often been described as the prettiest of the eleven girls in that family. She had large blue eyes, dimples, and beautiful curls. On her seventeenth birthday, she married Lyle Peterson, a young man who had worked for her father. They settled in Custer County, not far from the family homestead of my mother and Nina, but a long way from any medical care. After a couple of years Nina became pregnant, and she decided to have the baby delivered by a doctor in Gothenburg.

When labor pains began, Lyle put Nina in the car and started the long drive to Gothenburg. It was forty miles over hilly, rutted gravel roads. En route, Nina's water broke. When they finally reached the doctor's clinic, the doctor apparently panicked. He later told Nina's sister, Beulah, that he thought Nina was having twins, and fearing that second one was going to die in the womb, in his haste and confusion he pulled out Nina's female organs. The frightened doctor waited until that night to call in another doctor from North Platte, and by that time it was too late. Nina bled to death. The child, a daughter named Phyllis (after my mother), survived.

I learned early that death is part of life, but also that it is often inexplicable and never fully understandable. I think this view of death contributed to the freedom I enjoyed as a boy. It convinced us—my parents as well as me—that death is capricious and indiscriminate, and that being careful won't always defeat it. This may seem like a strange conclusion, because it's obvious now that some of our neighbors and relatives died because of carelessness, sometimes their own. But most of the deaths didn't appear avoidable to us at the time. Ernie Booth's employer didn't give him the option of not driving the tractor on the shoulder of a busy highway. The fathers of the neighbor boys killed in tractor or horse accidents needed their help, however dangerous the work was. Junior Dainton's death was too inexplicable to be blamed on carelessness. Bernie and Nina couldn't protect themselves against the negligence of the locomotive engineer and the doctor.

Rightly or wrongly, the conclusion we drew was that you never know when or how death will strike, so you might as well not worry about it. The illusion that everyone is entitled to live to a ripe old age didn't have much of a hold on us.

Me, post-puberty. I grew six
inches and filled out my t-shirt.

[20]

Swagger

BETWEEN ONE YEAR'S Lincoln County fair and the next, I crossed a watershed.

The fair was the payoff for a year's work raising an animal in 4-H Club. To a country kid, it was what Super Bowl week is to a football fan. We spent three or four days at the fairgrounds in North Platte, bedding down at night in the straw with our animals in the open-air livestock sheds. In that bedlam of kids and livestock and excitement, the 4-H leaders couldn't keep a close watch on us, so we had the run of the fairgrounds—the sounds and lights and thrills of the carnival, the smells of fresh produce and baked goods in the exhibit halls, the daytime stock car races and the evening variety shows in front of the grandstand.

The county fair was a first dip into a brand new universe of social possibilities for kids who had only known the dozen or so classmates at school. At the fair, we met strangers from other parts of the county, who seemed as exotic as foreigners. In obedience to that mysterious instinct that drives all children to practice the arts of social inclusion and exclusion, we formed shifting allegiances and enmities. We would prowl the midway with one set of new friends and then suddenly shun them for a new group—probably for no reason other than to shun them before they shunned us. For a few days, we felt free as grown-ups; we were actually freer, of course, but we were too young to understand that most adults aren't free at all.

The highlight of the last day of the fair was the boys' calf scramble. About a dozen 250-pound calves, and twice as many boys, were turned loose at the same time in the rodeo arena. A boy who could run down a calf, wrestle it to a standstill, put a halter on its head, and drag it across the finish line got to keep the calf.

I was first eligible for the calf scramble when I was twelve. For days, I chased calves in my dreams and envisioned myself winning a calf. By the time they released the calves I was beside myself with excitement. I ran around the arena like a dervish, looking for my opportunity. I never laid a hand on a calf. The boys who caught calves were those who lunged at them, got stepped on and dragged through the dirt, and eventually muscled a calf into submission. By the end I was dashing around the arena, panting, hoping vainly that some other boy would lose his grip, which would make his calf fair game for the rest of us.

On the ride home I was humiliated and ashamed. My parents did their best not to act disappointed, but I knew they knew what I also knew: I hadn't tried hard enough, hadn't wanted to catch a calf badly enough to take a chance, hadn't been aggressive enough to dive for a calf before some other boy could do so. Nancy said something about wishing they would let girls participate in the calf scramble, and I knew that if she had been entered she would have caught a calf, even though she was two years younger than I. I would have to endure another year of 4-H Club before I could redeem myself at the next calf scramble.

The 4-H Club provided some good times, such as the horse turd fight in the Tetros' corral, but it was mostly tedium. Every kid had a year-long project. Nancy and I raised breeding heifers—heifers destined to become mothers rather than hamburgers. We each started in the fall with a newly weaned six-month-old heifer and spent the next ten months feeding, grooming, doctoring, and training her to the halter. One of the goals of the 4-H clubs was to make agriculture more efficient and scientific. To that end, we had to keep meticulous records—the date the heifer was weaned, how much she was fed each day, what she weighed at various intervals, when we put weights on her horns and when we took them off. After a year of record-keeping and wrestling with heifers in snow and heat and mud, we presented them at the county fair to be judged against those of kids from other clubs throughout the county.

Nancy and I were never spectacularly successful with our breeding heifers. Neither of us shared Dad's penchant for record-keeping. The Grand Championships were always won by kids who took 4-H more seriously than we did. But we shampooed our heifers, fluffed their tails, and brushed their hair up so it made them look more perfect than they were. Nancy liked the primping, but she couldn't seem to avoid getting her toes under the heifer's feet. I have memories of Nancy with tears in her eyes, trying to get an eight-hundred-pound heifer to move off her foot. When our class was called to the show ring, we paraded our heifers before the judges. With our eyes we beseeched the judges for blue ribbons, but we usually collected red ones—meaning our heifers were good but not great.

In the year after my calf scramble failure, I raised another breeding heifer, filled out the endless feed and weight charts, carried grain and hay, broke the heifer to lead, and taught her to stand straight for the judges. And something else happened that year: puberty arrived and testosterone began its work. I grew six inches and filled out my t-shirt.

At the fair that August, I met a girl named Pat who was fifteen and had a curvaceous plump figure. She let me hold her hand and roam the midway with her. She was from the Hershey 4-H club at the other end of the county, which to me might as well have been Paris. The kids from Pat's club were sleeping in the bed of a stock truck rather than in the livestock sheds, and I persuaded her to let me sleep in the truck too. That turned out not to be a step up in the world of accommodations, because it drizzled during the night and the truck was open to the sky while the sheds were covered. But being chilly and wet was a small price to pay for the exhilaration of lying in the straw next to a strange girl who had curves.

I entered the calf scramble again, and Pat was there to watch. When they released the calves, I slammed into the nearest one, got him in a headlock with my right arm and fished the halter over his head with my left. I was the first boy to drag his calf across the finish line. What I felt wasn't vindication; the previous year's humiliation had been forgotten. I just felt satisfied. Of course I had caught a calf; why wouldn't I? The on-again, off-again self-confidence of adolescence, miserably absent the previous year, was in full swagger this year.

The calf I caught had been donated by the company owned by the mayor of North Platte, Kirk Mendenhall, whom we had read about in the North Platte newspaper because he had been elected on a promise to "clean up the town" (only much later did I learn that was the paper's euphemism for "close down the brothels"). I wrote the obligatory thank-you letter to Mr. Mendenhall. When he replied a few weeks later, I was awestruck to have received a personal letter from so august a figure as the mayor of North Platte.

The Anderson children at the Jacox
place, on my graduation from eighth
grade in 1952. Front row, from left:
Ellen, Elaine, and Walt. Back row:
Nancy and me. We moved away from the
Union community later that summer.

[21]

Off to See the World

IN THE SUMMER OF 1952 we moved away from Union for good. I had finished the eighth grade. If we had stayed at Union, I would have attended Brady High School, which was so small it could barely scrape up a six-man football team. There were only three students in my cousin Roger's Brady high school class. My parents wanted all their children to have the benefits of a bigger high school, so they bought a fine little farm on the north bank of the Platte River, just a mile from Gothenburg, and we all went to school there.

In the exciting new world of town school, I soon discovered that my rustic education in Union's one-room school had prepared me well. I excelled in classes, played football, was elected to student offices, won leading roles in class plays, and dated popular girls. My eyes began to open to the wider world.

When I turned sixteen, my parents sent me off to see some of that world. I went to Virginia to visit an uncle who was in the Navy there, spent a few days by myself in Washington, and visited a distant cousin in Chicago. I don't remember whether the initial idea was my parents' or mine. In either event, it was a remarkable thing for them to do, considering that neither of them had ever been east of Omaha and wouldn't have dreamed of spending that much money on travel for themselves.

My mother and father never burdened any of their children with the expectation that we should follow in their footsteps. That's surprising, because keeping the farm in the family was the usual ambition of the time. Some of my contemporaries were cursed with that—led to believe from birth that their destiny was to stay at home and eventually take over the farm or the ranch, no matter whether that suited their interests and aptitudes.

In my case, maybe my parents realized early on that I would have been a failure in that occupation. I could never keep my mind on the task at hand. To combat the boredom of riding the tractor, I worked long-division problems in my head when I was supposed to be counting the number of rows I had planted. If I was riding the fence looking for loose wires, I would find myself inventing verses to match the horse's rhythm instead of watching the passing fence. So what led my parents to send me on a trip may have been the desperate hope that I might find something I could do successfully.

The night before I was to leave, an evening in mid-June when the dusk seems to last forever, I was helping Dad in the shop. We were sharpening sickles, the moving part of the cutting bar on a mowing machine. One of my usual summer jobs after we moved near Gothenburg was mowing the prairie hay in the flat meadow that stretched all the way from our buildings to the Union Pacific railroad tracks. The hay was ready to cut, and I felt mildly guilty about leaving when my help was needed, but at age sixteen guilt is no match for excitement.

We were working close to the wide garage doors of the shop, salvaging the last lingering light. A soft summer wind was blowing in through the open doors, fireflies were courting in the tall native grass outside the shop, and Dad was telling me things a traveler would need to know:

"Don't keep all your money in one place. Don't leave a lot in your hotel room because all kinds of people have keys to your room. You can carry some in your shoe, but don't forget about it when you take off your shoes.

"You have to tip people who do things for you. You leave a few cents for the waiter after you pay the bill. When you check into a hotel you ought to be able to carry your own suitcases, but if they won't let you, you'll have to give the fella a dime or two.

"If you have to take a taxi, take one you've heard of. In the big cities some guys paint their cars up like taxis and then they pick people up and take 'em out and roll 'em.

"When you walk on the sidewalk in a big city, stay away from the doorways. If you're walking too close, somebody can reach out and grab you and nobody will even see it. If you walk on the edge by the street, at least you'll be out in the open.

"Stay out of the rough areas of town. As long as there are plenty of people around you'll probably be okay. Don't stay in a hotel you don't know anything about.

"Don't leave your belongings laying around. If you have to set something down, put it where you can keep an eye on it."

Hearing about all those hazards only raised my excitement. I wondered how Dad knew all those things, but I didn't doubt him because he always seemed to know things you wouldn't expect him to know. As I later came to appreciate, he was a man who learned a great deal from his experiences, limited as those might have been.

And I learned that evening of one experience Dad had never mentioned before. I knew that as a young man Dad loved baseball and was a good pitcher. What I hadn't known was that the summer after he graduated from high school, he rode freight trains to California. It was the beginning of the Great Depression, and he hoped to get paid to play ball, or at least get a paying job *and* play ball. I don't know whether he didn't mention it before because he thought it reflected badly on him, or because he didn't want to give me ideas.

He told me that evening how he had stayed awake all the first night, but then the second night had fallen asleep in a boxcar with some other men, and awoke in the night to see that a huge knife had fallen out of his neighbor's clothing and was lying between them, glistening in the moonlight.

"At least it looked huge to me. In them hard times lots of honest men rode the rails, and I hadn't thought about the chance that there might be some not so honest." He said he slept no more that night.

He knew little about the art of switching from one train to another to keep moving, and one night was stranded in Rock Springs, Wyoming. He and another rider made their way to the city park and were trying to sleep on park benches when a policeman roused them.

"He was a pretty decent fellow," Dad said. "He asked us where we was from and where we was going. He asked if we had any money and we said no. He said, 'Well, you can't sleep in the park. You come on with me and I'll let you sleep in the jail. It's warm there and in the morning you can go on your way.' So we spent the night in jail. I don't think they locked the doors. It was warmer in there, but I didn't sleep much. I guess I just didn't take to being in jail."

I asked Dad what he did when he got to California.

"Not much," he said. "I spent a day or two looking around, but I never even tried to get a job. I got on a freight and came home. I should've given it a try out there. I don't know why I didn't stay a while. Just homesick, I guess. You never know what might have happened if I had stuck it out."

By now it was too dark to see Dad's face, but I could hear a tangle of emotions in his voice. He was proud to have taken the trip, chagrined about having been in jail, and embarrassed at having hurried home. I detected the faintest strains of wanderlust in his words, a hint of longing—to be young and free, to go to faraway places and see strange things, to take chances and pursue dreams. Thoughts of that kind were a luxury he didn't often indulge. Never before or after did I heard him speak with emotion about his youth. I asked him about the California trip several times in later years, but his responses were matter-of-fact. The window of feeling that opened briefly on the eve of my trip was closed.

Willie Nelson once said his epiphany came as a boy when he was chopping cotton in the Texas summer and saw cars going by with their windows rolled up. The realization that some people were sitting in air conditioning while he sweltered in the sun made him aspire to something better. Mine came during those summers in the mid-50s when I was mowing hay in the meadow by the railroad tracks and saw the Union Pacific's famous domeliners flash past. I could catch a glimpse of nicely dressed people lifting a fork to their lips in the dining car, or people in the observation car gazing serenely over the passing countryside and the bumpkin mowing hay in the meadow.

The first leg of my journey was on one of those marvelous trains. I think it was *The City of San Francisco,* but it could have been *The City of Denver* or *The City of Los Angeles*. The year was 1955, and the high speed diesel trains, "streamliners," we called them, were the way to travel, at least across middle America.

The domeliners were the epitome of the streamliners. Each had an observation car, a double-decked coach car with a curved glass top that gave the top-deck passengers a view from above the rest of the train. Each domeliner also had a dining car with big picture windows, white tablecloths, and real silverware; a club car full of overstuffed lounge furniture, cigar smoke, and the tinkle of ice in glasses; at least one Pullman car with sleeping accommodations; and several coach cars with plush, roomy, comfortable reclining seats. The domeliners went almost a hundred miles an hour and all other trains got off the main track to make way for them.

The domeliners didn't even slow down for towns like ours. They stopped only at major towns like North Platte and Kearney, which are a hundred miles apart. My parents took me to North Platte, where I boarded the train in early evening. I was traveling coach class, of course. I spied an empty seat and hoisted my two huge, brand-new suitcases into the overhead racks. In the seat beside me was a woman. At the time she registered in my mind only as an older woman; now I would guess she was in her mid-twenties. Her name was Irene, and she was a schoolteacher in Indiana. She had been visiting a sister in Denver.

I looked out the window in awe as we picked up speed and began outracing the cars on the highway that paralleled the tracks. In no time at all Gothenburg flashed past; I had forgotten to watch for my hay field west of town. After a while I got up to go to the dining car and discovered that you have to walk like a drunken sailor to keep your balance. The doors between cars opened miraculously, and for the few seconds it took to move from one to the next, the heat and noise reminded me that this flying paradise really was just a train.

In the dining car I was served a sandwich by a stout black waiter wearing a white coat, who called me "Suh." I had never been called "sir"; in fact I don't think I had ever heard anyone called "sir." In our egalitarian culture, there was little need for titles more honorific than "Mister." I wondered why a middle-aged man was waiting tables. I had never seen waiters in the cafes at home, only waitresses, or maybe a high school boy too inept to get a real job.

But this man did not seem embarrassed about his job. Unlike the waitresses I had seen, who hurried about and always seemed harried, he moved with great deliberation, and his broad expressionless face conveyed a sense of dignity, if not superiority. I left a tip, probably ten or fifteen cents, and his "Thank you, suh, thank you" left me wondering whether he was expressing gratitude or condescension.

Back in my seat, I noticed a scent I didn't recognize. It wasn't perfume exactly, but it smelled soft and lovely, and it clearly came from Irene. She smiled at me, and asked about my trip, and what I did at home. When I told her I had spent the last week lifting hay bales onto a wagon, she said, "Ah, that's how you got those nice brown muscles."

She was friendly, and as we talked she would lean my way from time to time, so her bare arm touched mine. Soon my attention was all focused on her smell and her smile and her soft skin, and I forgot about the passing scenery. I had meant to go sit in the dome car before it got dark, but I didn't. I was aching to touch her, but terribly confused. She was a teacher, as old as some of my teachers, and I was not yet a high school junior. I couldn't believe she would let me touch her. But I had done some necking and petting with girls my age, and they had never seemed as willing as she did. I wondered what would happen to me if she screamed or complained to the conductor. But I had never felt such a powerful need for physical contact, so I crafted a plan. I would yawn and stretch, and then I would let my arm drop to the top of her seat. If she didn't seem to object to that, I might later let my arm drop around her shoulders, if the chance presented itself.

I got up my courage, stretched, and lowered my arm to the top of the seat. When I did, she snuggled against me, put her head on my chest, and put her arm around my waist. I was dumbfounded. Neither of us said a word, but she must have heard my heart pounding. She looked up at me and smiled, then put her head back on my chest.

We spent the night in that embrace. At some point a porter came through the train offering blankets, and Irene asked for one. We spread it over the two of us. After a while, under the blanket I put my hand on her breast. She shifted her body a little, but she didn't object. I stayed awake all night, touching her breasts from time to time. When she awoke in the morning, my hand was there. She looked at me with a slightly surprised smile and I hastily withdrew my hand. She snuggled against me for a few more minutes before we arrived at Union Station.

When the train stopped there was sudden pandemonium. Everybody jumped up and began pulling luggage down from the racks. I got Irene's suitcases down for her, and when I got my two suitcases in hand it was impossible for us to even stand close to each other. She stepped off the train first, and when I came down the steps she put down her bags, took my face in her hands and kissed me. I had a suitcase in each hand.

"You're sweet," she said. She hurried away and I never saw her again.

Union Station was beautiful. It had the highest ceiling I had ever seen, and was crowded with hurrying people. I found a locker for my suitcases, had a cup of coffee and some toast in the station coffee shop, and bought a *Life* magazine. I had to change stations because my ticket from Chicago to Virginia was on the Baltimore and Ohio, or some such line, that didn't operate out of Union Station. But I had most of the day to spend in Chicago. My first project was to telephone my Dad's cousin, Clare Babe, and her husband, Fred, to confirm that I would visit them on my return from the East Coast.

I found some phone booths on the second floor beside a great marble staircase. There was a wide marble balustrade around the staircase, just outside the phone booths. I had to get out a piece of paper with the phone number because I had never had to dial a number with so many digits—at home we had just four. I laid the *Life* magazine on the balustrade so I could hold my dime in one hand and the paper in the other. Just as Aunt Clare answered, I saw a big black hand come over the top of the ledge and descend down the stairs with my magazine. Too late I remembered Dad's warning: "Don't leave your belongings laying around."

I was beginning to feel a little rattled by my experiences as a traveler, so I decided that rather than spend the day sightseeing, I would just go to the B&O station and take it easy until my train left that night. I got my suitcases out of the locker and lugged them for what seemed like half a mile to one of the station's entrances.

There was a long line of taxis waiting at the curb. The first one was a black car with something like "Joe's Taxi" painted on the side. The second one was a yellow Checker cab with the black and white checkerboard pattern that was familiar even in Nebraska. Remembering Dad's warning about no-name taxis whose drivers take their passengers out and roll them, I headed for the Checker.

The driver was beginning to tell me something about "first in line" when the driver of the Joe's Taxi opened his door and began yelling something in our direction. I didn't hear it, but it caused my driver to get out of his cab and start yelling at Joe. I heard him say, "I told him that." Joe got out and came back to my driver, still yelling, and gave him a little push in the chest. My driver grabbed Joe by the shirt front and pushed him up against the cab. Joe took a swing at my driver but missed.

I grabbed my suitcases and ran back into the station. As I ran I heard more yelling and then a thump, like a body slamming into the side of a car. I hurried straight through the station to the entrance on the opposite side and took the first cab in line.

The B&O station (if that's what it was) was smaller, older, and more run-down. I tried to sleep but too many emotions were jostling me. In late afternoon I began to think about spending another night without sleep. I thought about the Pullman cars, and how wonderful it would be to sleep through the night in a comfortable bed. I inquired about the options, and learned that the cheapest was a "roomette," a small compartment with a fold-down bed. The cost was enormous— over a hundred dollars as I recall. I had the money, but if I spent it for the roomette I would have to ask my parents for more before the trip was over. But my nerves were frayed and I soon persuaded myself that it would be money well spent.

I sat up in my roomette and watched some ugly parts of the city slide by while the train pulled out of Chicago, but as soon as it began to get dark I pulled down the bed and slept soundly. I awoke briefly in the middle of the night when my car was switched to a different train in Cincinnati, but went back to sleep as soon as we were moving again.

When I awoke in the early morning, I thought for a minute I had died. We were rolling through mountains covered with forests the likes of which I had never seen. The air seemed to be full of something finer than mist, more uniform than steam, and less dense than fog. In the few places where the early morning sun was able to penetrate the forest, it fired golden shafts through the liquid air. In many places the ground and the underbrush were entirely covered by vines. The scene was so ethereal I thought for a minute I must be in heaven.

We came to a town, the most old-fashioned town I had ever seen. The cars all seemed to be Model A's or even older, the streets were mud, and most of the houses were unpainted. But it was a bustling town, with men in overalls on the streets and cars lined up at the crossing waiting for our train to pass. I later deduced that we must have been in West Virginia, passing through the Appalachian Mountains or maybe the Great Smokies. I had the sense that I had passed into a different world.

My destination was Williamsburg, Virginia. My uncle Richard Bailey, eight or ten years my elder, was stationed at the Norfolk naval base. He and his wife Joann lived in a trailer on the outskirts of Williamsburg. I had never seen so much color. There were flowers everywhere—in the trailer park, in the town, along the highways. There were hollyhocks around many of the trailers. For the first time I saw whole trees covered with blossoms; I found out they were called crepe myrtles. There were trees with huge white blossoms—magnolias, I learned. Here too I felt like I was in a strange and beautiful new land.

Richard and Joann took me to Virginia Beach to see the ocean. We waded in the surf and then I decided to walk out farther. I was in water about waist deep when a wave hit me and knocked me head over heels. I was awestruck by the power of the water, and it seemed like minutes passed before the wave let me surface.

I cherished my few days with Richard and Joann, people of my place and blood who just happened to be living in paradise. Richard was an engineer who worked a five-day week for the Navy. They lived a simple and comfortable life surrounded by beauty and history. My days there were a serene antidote to the hyper-excitement of the train trip.

But the adolescent psyche recovers quickly, and when it was time for me to go to Washington I was ready for more adventure. On the train approaching Washington, I saw a billboard for the Pennsylvania Hotel. The picture showed a substantial brick building and the sign said "reasonable rates," so when I arrived in Washington I told the cab driver to take me to the Pennsylvania Hotel. Through pure luck, it turned out to be a suitable place. It was on the edge of a deteriorating neighborhood not too far from the Capitol and the other places I wanted to visit. It was a little past its prime, but it was clean and I didn't feel unsafe.

The hotel had an old-fashioned elevator, the kind surrounded by brass gates and operated by a uniformed man. After I checked in, the bellman grabbed my suitcases before I could pick them up and led me to the elevator. My room was on the sixth or seventh floor. After the bellman installed me in my room I tipped him, I think with two dimes, and I wondered if I should have tipped the elevator operator.

After unpacking my things, I realized I should have bought a newspaper so I would know if there were any special events I might be able to see. So I went back down to the lobby and this time I tipped the elevator man a nickel. That seemed to please him, so when I went back up I tipped him another nickel.

After an hour or so of studying the newspaper and my travel brochures, I developed a craving for a candy bar. So I went back down to the lobby and when the operator let me out of the elevator I found that I had no change. He looked hurt when I walked away without tipping him, so when I went back up I tipped him a quarter. That pleased him greatly, but I then began to realize that if I tipped him every trip I would run short of money. The price of the newspaper was five cents but with tips it had cost me fifteen, and the five-cent candy bar had cost me thirty cents.

For a while I stayed in my room to avoid the problem. Then it occurred to me to go to the lobby, wait for some other people, get on the elevator with them, and see if they tipped when they got out. I tried it but it didn't work. The other people who got on were going to a higher floor and the operator let me out first. I got off without tipping him and decided then and there that I wouldn't do so any more. After that he seemed perplexed and I felt terrible, so I tried to make as few trips on the elevator as I could.

The next day I took a Gray Line tour of Washington. There were to be stops at the Capitol, the White House, and the Museum of Science and Industry, but the first stop was the National Gallery. First we came to a garden room, with a high vaulted glass ceiling and trees growing indoors! There was so much greenery, natural light, and burbling water it was hard to believe I was inside a building. Then we came to the rotunda, and I was dumbstruck. It was surrounded by a dozen or more black marble columns, four feet in diameter and twenty-five or thirty feet tall. Designs were inlaid in the marble floor, and in the center was a massive fountain topped by a bronze statue of Mercury—with uncovered genitals! But what overwhelmed me was the soaring dome. It seemed as if it might pull me off the floor and make me soar too. I had never imagined a building could have such an effect on the psyche.

I stayed there, absorbing the majesty and serenity of the place. Some of my tour companions came by and said the bus was leaving, but I let it leave without me. I stayed so long that a guard asked if I was all right. I ventured into one or two of the wings of the building and tried to look at the statues and paintings, but the rotunda kept pulling me back. I stayed until closing time, and then I walked back to the hotel.

I remember little about the rest of the trip. Fred and Clare, my relatives in Chicago, lived near Wrigley Field and Fred took me to a Cubs game. They showed me Lake Michigan but I was not impressed; I had seen the ocean. I encountered no more Irenes.

As soon as I got home I went to work in the wheat harvest for a friend of Dad's named Bud. The job was near Maywood, forty miles from home. My job was to drive a two-ton Diamond T truck across the fields to the combine, where Bud pumped wheat from the combine into the truck. When the truck got full I had to hurry to the buildings, unload the wheat, and get back before Bud was ready to dump the next load from the combine.

About the second day I broke an axle trying to shift gears too quickly while crossing loose plowed ground. Because it was an old, odd-ball truck, a new axle had to be shipped from Omaha. In the meantime we used the truck as a trailer, pulling it with a tractor and a log chain. When the truck got full Bud had to get off the combine and drive the tractor while I steered the truck. We couldn't maneuver it into position to unload by raising the truck box, so I had to feed the grain into the elevator with a scoop shovel. This slowed the harvest considerably, which was no small matter to Bud, because delay can mean loss of the crop if a hailstorm hits before the wheat is harvested.

Bud didn't blame me for the broken axle, and he was apologetic about my having to scoop the wheat. But I knew I had been more trouble than help, and I felt terrible. The weather was scorching and I was sweating through my clothes and drinking too much sweetened ice tea, which gave me a bad case of hives. After a few days Bud suggested in as kindly a way as possible that I go home. Humiliated but grateful and relieved, I went.

If I had returned from the east coast to something I liked—branding, for example—the trip might have gradually faded into distant memory, like a pleasant vacation. But there in the wheat field, sweating and itching and failing, my compass turned forever from the life I had known to the one I had glimpsed.

*"To combat the boredom of riding
the tractor, I worked long-division
problems in my head when I was
supposed to be counting the number
of rows I had planted." Above: Me,
ready to do some plowing, circa 1952.*

[22]

Emerging Ambitions

DURING THE NEXT SCHOOL YEAR, I read about the National High School Institute at Northwestern University. It offered a program for high school students in the summer before their senior year. I applied for the science program, and to my surprise, I was admitted.

The Institute was a mix of coursework, field trips, and social events. The classes in math, physics, and chemistry pushed me to my limits, if not beyond. The trips were exciting. We went to the Argonne National Laboratory, where scientists were engaged in some of the most advanced nuclear technology of the time. We went to some other laboratory, where we saw an early computer in operation, powered by an entire room full of radio tubes. The burning debate of the time was whether the future lay with analog or digital computers. The scientists we talked to were betting on analog.

We went to a White Sox game at Comiskey Park, listened to a concert in Grant Park, and went to an ice show in the Boulevard Room of the Conrad Hilton Hotel. For a country kid from Nebraska, it was a dazzling experience.

Evanston in midsummer was lush. The boys lived in McCormick Hall, on Lake Michigan at the very water's edge. Some evenings I sat alone on the dock and watched the moon make dancing golden ringlets on the water. The air was soft and moist as the breath of a beautiful girl. There was one of those too, dark-haired, tanned, shapely, and poised as a princess. Her name was Betsy Little and she was from Middletown, Ohio. The next year when I first saw Natalie Wood, I thought she was the only woman in the world who might be as lovely as Betsy Little. Every boy in the science program was in love with Betsy, and most of the college guys too.

As time began to run out, hope and desperation triumphed over fear and embarrassment, and I asked her for a date. I think it was to attend a play, *Miss Lonelyhearts,* starring Pat O'Brien. It was an outing for the entire group, of course, and Betsy seemed uncertain about just what a date would mean under those circumstances. I was too paralyzed to say I would be ecstatic if she would just sit beside me. I just turned away, my fragile moment of courage shattered.

Parents were invited to attend the final banquet, and mine came. I was surprised; it should have been even harder than usual for them to get away, because I hadn't been home to help with the work for much of the summer.

Neither of them had ever been farther east than Omaha. They were as wide-eyed and excited as I had been when I arrived four weeks earlier. They were good-looking, self-conscious about their country manners, but proud and unapologetic. I was proud of them. Dean Seulberger, the director of the Institute, went out of his way to make them comfortable. He showed them around the campus and treated them like guests of honor.

At the banquet, a few scholarships were to be awarded to the best students of the Institute. I had little hope of winning one. The math classes had eventually moved out of my range, and my results in the chemistry lab never quite matched the ideal. But we had taken a battery of aptitude tests early on, and apparently those figured heavily in the award of scholarships. To my amazement, my name was called and I went to the front of the room to be congratulated by Dean Seulberger and offered a full scholarship to Northwestern University for four years. As I returned to my seat, Betsy Little smiled at me.

We stayed on for a day or two, sightseeing in Chicago. In the lives of children and parents, dependency moves from the former to the latter in innumerable tiny steps. Some of the earliest I remember occurred then; I found myself explaining to my parents why the heart of Chicago is called the Loop, showing them how to buy tickets for the El, introducing them to the novelty of pedestrian lights that allowed people to cross an intersection in all directions at once. For many years, my parents referred to that as their trip "back East."

My parents later told me that before the banquet, Dean Seulberger had "called long distance" to say that I was to be awarded a scholarship and that he personally would like them to be there. That, together with the gracious treatment he gave them while they were in Evanston, made my mother and father unshakable fans of Northwestern.

For me, though, other ambitions were emerging. For one thing, I was losing my zeal for science. Roles in several high school plays stimulated my interest in the humanities. And I discovered Walt Whitman and Ernest Hemingway and Sigmund Freud. At Northwestern, I had learned that while the world admires scientists, it doesn't love them. It was clear that the science students were the social misfits of the Institute. Except for Betsy, all the good-looking girls were in the other programs—journalism, music, and drama. On our joint excursions the other kids, girls and boys alike, shunned the science kids. They were cool, we were weird. I decided I wanted to be a psychiatrist, not a scientist.

After I won the scholarship to Northwestern, received my scores on the College Board exams, and was named one of the state winners of the Westinghouse Science Talent Search, I started getting letters from colleges all over the country. Some just invited me to apply, but others offered admission and scholarships. In my naiveté, that emboldened me to think about grander possibilities. I kept the letters, and I see now that they were from places like St. John's College and Wilmington Institute. But I knew little about the pecking order of colleges, and if one faraway school wanted me, why not another?

I decided that if I could go anywhere I wanted, it would be Harvard, only because that was the grandest and most impossible goal I could imagine. As I read Harvard's peculiarly arch literature and imagined life as one of the great intellectuals that it seemed to unfailingly produce, it became not just a pipe dream, but a real aspiration—not a realistic hope, but a secret and unspeakable dream, which if denied would leave no hurt but if fulfilled would be better than admission to Heaven.

With May came decision time, and I must have allowed some hope to creep in, because I was watching the mail closely. We lived only a mile from town and our mailbox was at the edge of town. Each day at lunch I borrowed a bicycle and rode out to the mailbox.

One day there was a letter from Harvard. I tore it open and read the opening line: "It is a pleasure . . . ." My eyes raced past the rest of that paragraph, because I knew that unless I received a scholarship, admission would be just a cruel taunt.

The second paragraph said, "I am happy to tell you also that the Committee has voted to award you a Regional Scholarship . . . ."

In an instant my life had veered off in an entirely new direction, and I knew it. I could scarcely imagine where it was headed, but it was already exhilarating. I felt like I was standing at the edge of the universe, poised to experience all its wonders.

I pedaled maniacally back to school and announced the news to my girlfriend. She would be staying in Nebraska, and somehow I had overlooked the possibility that she might not share my joy at the prospect of my going two thousand miles away. She tried hard to make her congratulations sound sincere, but the cloud in her eyes betrayed her.

She was the first of many who found it hard to understand my ecstasy. When I told my parents, "I'm going to Harvard," it was clear they were more enthusiastic about my being admitted there than about my actually going.

When he realized I really planned to go, Dad said, "Don't you think we ought to talk this over?"

"Talk what over?" I said. "It's Harvard. Of course I'm going."

"But we don't know anything about it. Are you sure you know what you're getting into? What about Northwestern?"

"Dad, I've been admitted to *Harvard*. They're giving me a scholarship. It's good for all four years. And a part-time job. You won't have to pay for it. I'm going."

To their credit, they never argued against it again, though I know they wished many times that I was going to Northwestern, where they knew the nice Dean Seulberger would look out for me.

My teachers were proud that I had been accepted at Harvard, but they too weren't sure I should actually go there. Most graduates of Gothenburg High didn't go to college, and of those who did, most went to nearby schools like Kearney State Teachers College or Hastings

College or Nebraska Wesleyan. The most ambitious few went to the University of Nebraska. I later did a little research and learned that one other Gothenburg boy, son of the richest man in town, had gone to Harvard, but that was fifty years earlier and he didn't come back, so there was no living memory of such a thing.

The teachers had come to terms with my going to Northwestern. For them, as for my parents, that was within the realm of comprehension, barely. At least Illinois was in a place some of us had visited, or at least had relatives. I didn't know anyone who had ever been to Boston, and Massachusetts seemed only slightly less remote than Madagascar.

If I had been able then to fully appreciate the cultural distance between the Platte Valley and Harvard, I would have had more sympathy for the reservations my parents and teachers felt. But in my head I was already too big for the world I had known, and whether I was big enough for the one I was headed for never crossed my mind.

I spent the summer blissfully suspended between those worlds. I got a job with an alfalfa dehydrating mill, operating a machine that chopped the hay in the field and blew it into a truck. I worked twelve hours a day, seven days a week, in fields miles from town. The mill operated around the clock, and crews alternated monthly between day and night shift.

For two of the three months I worked the night shift, six to six, and I loved it. Off toward the Colorado border, dry lightning flashed most every night as the day's heat escaped from the plains. Some nights there were real thunderstorms, which occasionally drenched us but more often only spawned chilly winds.

The real marvel, though, was the sunrise. Just as dusk lingered for hours after sunset, so the dawn came on imperceptibly, reluctantly, teasingly. The first light was so subtle that sometimes I thought I was imagining it. But after a while the brightening would be unmistakable, and then the slow ballet of colors would begin. Unlike the strong yellows and reds of sunset, colors of sunrise were delicate and unfamiliar— the palest of lavenders, vague violets and purples. If the colors of sunset were those of heat and blood, the colors of sunrise were those of sublime joy and heartbreak. They left me with incomprehensible feelings of wonder and longing.

There was nothing aesthetically exquisite about the human side of working at the mill. It was as far as I've ever been from the world of achievement, hope, and stability. As I've already said, the hay mills were the employers of last resort. The work was seasonal, so it necessarily attracted those who didn't have a year-round job. A few college-bound kids worked for the mills as truck drivers from time to time, but I was the only one in any job at my mill and, to my knowledge, the only one working as a chopper operator at any of the mills.

The other two chopper operators in my crew were middle-aged men. One of them was a decent man with a nagging wife and a car full of kids, the sort who works hard but seems to be destined to always be barely hanging on. I rode once in his old car, and I would not otherwise know how many odors can be stored up over many years of sweaty bodies, sick kids, and wet diapers.

The other chopper operator, Chester, was a drunk and a whiner. His life was full of misfortunes, one of which was his wife, who was reputed to be a whore. He could find someone else to blame for all except the wife. He didn't like anybody, but he especially disliked me. His chopper broke down twice as often as mine. He thought it was because I had been given a newer machine that should have gone to him; the rest of us thought it was because he was too lazy or hung-over to grease all the bearings as we were supposed to do at the beginning of each shift.

As the summer wore on, he began blaming me for everything that went wrong. One night shortly after dark he tried to turn his rig too sharply and got the tongue of the chopper caught in the tractor wheel. The foreman and a couple of truck drivers were already surveying the damage when I got there.

As I approached, Chester exploded. "Goddamnit, you caused this. I'd 'a had plenty of room to turn if you'd 'a pulled your goddamn rig outta the way like you're supposed to."

The next thing I knew I was sitting astraddle him in the hay stubble bashing his face with my fist. The other guys pulled me off and later said it looked like I was going to kill him.

I once heard somebody say, "If you have to think about whether you want to fight, don't do it." That night was the only time in my adult life I didn't have to think about it.

The foreman sent Chester home for the night. We got his rig out of the way and went back to work. A couple of hours later—about closing time for the bars—I saw Chester's gray Plymouth drive into the field with the lights off. I was on the far side of the field, but as I continued to cut around the rectangle I would soon be on his side. I wasn't afraid of Chester, but what if he had brought back some of his friends? I pondered whether he had any friends. Then a scarier thought entered my mind: What if he's come back with a gun? I was sitting in the open, high atop the tractor, silhouetted no doubt by the bright running lights of the rig.

As I came around the side closest to Chester's car, I held my breath; the hair on my neck stood up. I remember wondering, if you're hit, do you hear the shot? But nothing happened, and I began to breathe again.

As I circled around the field, I saw that the car was still there. It occurred to me that maybe Chester was trying to screw up his courage or steady his hand enough to get off an accurate shot. Or maybe he was out of the car, advancing in the dark to get a closer shot.

I held my breath through two or three more passes, and then I watched the car drive slowly and silently all the way around the perimeter of the field. Finally it drove away, still with the lights out.

Chester quit before the next night shift and I never saw him again.

Working the night shift wasn't as tough on my social life as you might think. In fact, the day shift was worse; if you have to get up at five in the morning to get to work by six, and you don't get off work until twelve hours later, it's hard to enjoy your evenings. But when you're working in the fields sometimes you get rained out, and if you've slept all day and have all the next day to sleep too, you own those nights. I was dating two girls, neither of whom was at liberty to stay out all night. But sometimes I persuaded them to push their midnight curfews a little toward dawn by reminding them that if it didn't rain again I wouldn't have another night off all summer.

Ready to go off to college,
in my North Platte fashions.

[23]

Bumpkin at Harvard

WHEN SEPTEMBER CAME my mother and father drove me to Kearney to catch the train to Boston. Kearney was a hundred miles farther east than North Platte, and that saved a dollar or two off the cost of the ticket. My mother told me many years later, "We both cried a little on the way home." They understood, as parents do, that the boy they knew would never be back.

I arrived in Boston after a thirty-six-hour train trip that inexplicably detoured across part of Canada, where a stranger shared his Canadian whisky with me in the club car. In my two big new imitation leather suitcases I had a couple of sport coats that were the latest fashion in North Platte, a few skinny neckties, and a shiny new pair of shoes that closed with a hinged tongue rather than laces.

I took a taxi from the train station. The streets were chaotic. Streetcars, trackless trolleys, buses, and cars all seemed to be competing for what little space there was. I learned later that you could reach Harvard by a pleasant drive along the Charles River, but the taxi went all the way via Massachusetts Avenue, a route that revealed all the gritty reality of an overcrowded city.

After what must have been close to an hour, the driver said, "Okay, this is Harvard Square, where do we go from here?"

All I saw were filthy streets converging from all directions, sooty business buildings, a maze of trolley wires overhead, cars and pedestrians everywhere. In the middle of it all, squeezed by traffic on all sides, was a newsstand and subway entrance.

My physical expectations of Harvard had been formed entirely by the few photographs I had seen in Harvard's literature—pictures of thoughtful-looking scholars striding across a peaceful Harvard Yard, or photos taken from the south side of the Charles River looking across the grassy banks of the river at the fine red brick Houses, with their clean white bell towers and spires thrusting above the leafy surroundings.

"I don't think this is right," I told the driver. "Harvard is on a river. We need to look for a campus."

"No, kid, this is Harvard. All this, it's all Harvard. Now what building are we looking for?"

Eventually we found the right entrance to the Yard, and in it the dormitory to which I was assigned.

The Yard *was* a place of relative tranquility, but only in comparison to the bedlam outside its walls. I never got used to the noise of the city—the shouts and honking of horns at all hours, sirens in the night, the constant revving, rumbling, and screeching of traffic. My ears were tuned to the sounds of wind, cattle, frogs, owls, and coyotes.

For the part-time job that was to make up the difference between my scholarship and my expenses, I had a choice between working in the freshman dining hall and working on the dorm crew, which cleaned other freshmen's rooms. I chose the latter, in part because it paid five cents an hour more, but mainly because I didn't want to be a waiter to my classmates.

The dorm crew was required to report a week ahead of everybody else to get the rooms ready for occupancy. That first week we vacuumed and scrubbed all day, and at night we explored Cambridge and Boston. We quickly found the places that would serve us alcohol. We brazenly, but entirely hypothetically, negotiated prices with the streetwalkers on Columbus Avenue. All of us were scholarship students, mostly from the Midwest or West, and we quickly developed a boot-camp style of camaraderie.

After the other students arrived and classes started, the pleasure of being on dorm crew soon vanished. For one thing, our jobs made us a conspicuous minority group. Each of us was either on the wet crew or the dry crew. If you were wet, each day you went to the dorm crew headquarters, checked out a mop, mop pail, and spray tank, carried the paraphernalia across the Yard to the dorm you were assigned to clean, spent two hours scrubbing bathrooms, and then carried the equipment back across the Yard. If you were dry, it was a vacuum cleaner that you carried.

As I began getting acquainted with other students in my classes and my dorm, meeting them while I was carrying my janitorial equipment became an acute embarrassment. I thought it instantly branded me in their eyes as a scholarship student, a poor kid who didn't really belong at Harvard but had been let in as part of a misguided egalitarian experiment. Of course all those things would have been clear to them anyway—from my dress, my accent, and my body language—but I didn't realize that then.

The other misfortune of being on dorm crew was that we learned too much about the personal habits of our peers. They knew which day their rooms would be cleaned, they knew the dorm crew was not expected to move personal belongs, and they knew the person doing the cleaning was a classmate, but many of them left their rooms a mess. Floors were strewn with half-eaten pizzas and discarded clothes, books, and newspapers. Bathrooms were littered with toilet paper, dirty underwear, and soggy towels. My assignments were in several different dormitories, and I observed that the filthiest rooms were often in the most expensive dorms.

I had little previous exposure to sloth, or the other manifestations of thoughtless arrogance by privileged young people. I was appalled that students would dart across Massachusetts Avenue in mid-block, forcing drivers to choose between stopping or running them down. Once, in a men's room at the undergraduate library, I noticed that the guy in the next stall had spread the *Harvard Crimson* on the floor and seemed to be reading it. To my amazement, when he departed he simply left it there. Didn't it occur to him that the next person using the stall would have to walk across his discarded newspaper? Didn't he realize someone eventually would have to pick it up? In the Scandinavian precincts of the Midwest, we believed no one should take up more than his share of space on earth—a view not widely embraced at Harvard.

I would like to be able to say that observing the bad behavior of my classmates gave me a sense of moral superiority, but it didn't. It just convinced me that I was naïve and foolish, and soon I too was behaving with Ivy League arrogance.

Walking the streets of Cambridge and Boston, I learned the most depressing fact about city life: people won't speak to you. In Brady or Gothenburg—even in North Platte, where I knew no one and no one knew me—anyone you met on the street greeted you with a smile, a wave, or at least a nod, and said "Hi" or "Good morning" or "Nasty wind today, isn't it?"

In Boston I began to wonder if I was invisible. People walked past without even glancing my way, or worse, looked right through me. I was bewildered, then angered, then saddened. Even now, after a lifetime of city life, it still rankles when I meet someone on the sidewalk, with no one else in sight, and the person stares ahead as if to deny my existence. I know the excuses—if you make eye contact the person may mug you or rape you—but they don't make me less sad. If we made a habit of acknowledging our common humanity, maybe we wouldn't have to worry so much about being mugged or raped.

That was all part of learning about the world, of course. All young people need to reinvent themselves. To grow up is to recognize the shackles we wear by virtue of family, heritage, convention, and geography. Any alert adolescent comes to resent the banality of his or her inherited world, its willingness to trade possibility for stability, the readiness to compromise, and especially the eagerness of the adult world to impose those traits on the young. My friends and I were so far from home, culturally as well as geographically, that our heritage exerted little gravitational pull. The challenge we faced now was to choose a new persona without ending up completely adrift.

I had come from a world that disapproved of aspiring to be better than others, where use of too many multi-syllable words was a social gaffe, where "the north end of a south wind is always cold" was considered a wise observation. That value system wasn't easy to square with the one in which I now found myself.

I don't think it was such a big problem for classmates whose aspirations were totally intellectual. For them Harvard was an unmixed blessing. Probably for the first time in their lives, they had plenty of like-minded companions and enough stimulation to keep their minds working at full capacity all the time.

For those of us who aspired to be "well rounded," it wasn't so simple. We wanted to do well academically, but we also wanted to be socially adept, play sports, win girls, and be admired by men. Those of us for whom the trip to Harvard was a long one really *were* reinventing ourselves, and it wasn't easy to know how far to go.

I had one friend who erased all traces of his previous life. He was a gangly kid from South Dakota, son of a merchant and graduate of a public high school. On arrival at Harvard, he set about transforming himself. Within a few weeks he was showing the rest of us how to line up the stripes on a rep tie, how to recognize a Brooks Brothers suit, how to tell genuine cordovan shoes from others that are merely cordovan-colored. He bought an umbrella and a chesterfield coat, used a cigarette holder, drank sherry, and cultivated a vaguely British-sounding accent. By the end of freshman year, he was the preppiest of preppies, and would have nothing to do with his rustic former friends.

I often wondered what they would make of him if he went back to South Dakota. I suppose he never did, at least until he could go there as a stranger no longer at risk of meeting up with his old self.

Another friend, also from the plains, chose the opposite route. He didn't adapt at all. He wore unpressed pants an inch or two too short, white or colored socks, and penny loafers. His hair was an ill-kempt version of Frankie Avalon's. He talked like a guy who was still trying to find the load of pumpkins. Worst of all, he couldn't, or wouldn't, adapt his body movements to the possible presence of other persons or objects. He was a big loud friendly geek who bumbled around Harvard like it was a shipyard. I was as embarrassed by (and for) him as I was bemused by my phony preppy friend.

I adapted a little. I put away my lever-action shoes, bought a couple of tweed "natural shoulder" (i.e., no pads) sport coats from the Harvard Coop to supplement my North Platte fashions, and stopped calling the midday meal dinner. But I refused to swap my Wranglers for chinos and I didn't give up my flattop haircut.

For me the biggest problem was maintaining some connection between my old world and this new one. My place, my experiences, my past, seemed to be simply irrelevant. For that matter, so was I. Harvard was full of bright eighteen-year-olds, many of them smarter and more talented than I.

So far as I could tell, the Great Plains had contributed nothing to American history that mattered here. At home we thought the covered wagons, the Pony Express, the homesteaders, and the transcontinental railroad were important. Here those were just colorful anecdotes, not part of anything really *historical.* The nation known to the Harvard community lay between New England, Washington, and Chicago.

In the same way that a Briton at the height of the empire would have been aware of Canada and India, Harvard people were aware that there were provinces in California and the South. A few of the outlying states (Texas, for example) were exotic enough to arouse some curiosity. Even Oklahoma could do so, because the Rodgers and Hammerstein musical of that name had just been made into a hit movie. But Nebraska was simply unknown. I don't remember anyone expressing any interest in what it was like. No one seemed to know, or care, where it was. My answer to the obligatory where-are-you-from question usually produced only a blank look, but once a classmate brightened and said, "Oh, I've been there. I went a couple of years ago with my family. We visited Hoover Dam and Lake Mead."

My classes—chemistry, calculus, and classical literature—were all challenging, but my beginning French course was a nightmare. The professor who taught it was one of the originators of the theory that adults should learn languages as children do, by speaking it. So every minute of the course was conducted in French—not only the instruction, but also the announcements, assignments, and directions. That we couldn't understand them because we didn't *know* any French wasn't considered a serious obstacle. It was like learning to swim by being thrown in the pool.

Two days a week the professor lectured, entirely in French, to the whole class of two or three hundred students. The third meeting of the week was a section meeting of twelve or fifteen students, taught by a graduate student who drilled us individually or in small groups on what we were supposed to have learned in the lectures.

My section teacher was a haughty and impatient Parisienne. She believed the French language was a thing of beauty and elegance, not to be defiled by American accents. She assumed we could learn vocabulary and grammar from the books and lectures; her job was to teach us pronunciation. When we mispronounced her beloved mother tongue, she rolled her eyes, sighed, groaned, scowled, shook her head, waved her arms, stamped, and raged.

For reasons I still don't understand, most people were able to learn French by this method. At least in my section, students were so intimidated by the mademoiselle that they even learned what sounded to my ears like pretty good French pronunciation. But not me.

"Monsieur Onderso!" It always took me a second or two to realize that meant me. "Dites vous, 'ou.'"

"Ou," I replied. Only I suppose it came out more like "Ooo."

"Non! Non! Non! C'est 'ou.'"

I would try again. "Ou." I suppose now it came out something like "oooi."

"Monsieur Onderso. Ecoute: 'ou.'"

It was hopeless. For the first time in my life, I was the class dolt. The mademoiselle would come to my seat, thrust her face in front of mine, and try to show me how to form my lips, how to place my tongue on my teeth. I would try, and she would despair. But she wouldn't give up. Every week we joined up for two hours of misery. It must have been as frustrating for her as it was humiliating for me.

That Thursday afternoon French section became the defining point of my week. By Tuesday I would begin feeling weak in the stomach. By Wednesday I had sweaty palms and couldn't sleep. I couldn't go to my Thursday morning classes because I was in a panic about my French section. When it was over, I was too mired in despair, humiliation, and self-loathing to face anyone for the rest of that day. By Friday I could push French into the back of my mind and think about the weekend. But the next Tuesday it started all over again.

Part of my problem may have been that I couldn't even pronounce

English, at least not in any way that the mademoiselle would have recognized. In my native tongue, your mother's sister is an ant. You mail a letter in an invilope. Guests are cumpney. So mebby it's jist not sprisin' I couldn't pernounce 'ou.'" Er learn Frinch eether.

Those weekly sessions assaulted my manhood as well as my intellectual self-respect. The mademoiselle was not more than four or five years older than I was. She was beautiful and excitingly, foreignly sexy. At a time when American women were tightly packaged in panty girdles and stiff bras, she wore clinging jersey dresses that rippled and jiggled. She wore spike heels that clicked erotically as she strode down the aisle to humiliate me. Her big hoop earrings dangled in my face. She had round brown eyes and long dark eyelashes. She demonstrated proper linguistic techniques a foot from my face, pursing her full ripe lips and curling her lovely tongue. Perhaps it is not surprising that I wasn't picking up the nuances of forming diphthongs. At the time, however, the fact that my nightmares were caused by someone who could have been a source of delicious fantasies only intensified my misery.

Trying to learn French without benefit of English was only slightly more daunting than trying to date without a car. I had started driving a car at fourteen, having learned on tractors and trucks long before that, so I had never experienced carless dating. I was willing to assume that it was possible, because hardly anyone at Harvard had a car. But I soon learned that it isn't, at least not in a form that would be recognized as a real date by any red-blooded American from west of the Mississippi.

Dating Radcliffe women was out of the question because we outnumbered them four-to-one and the few good-looking ones were instantly snapped up by upperclassmen. Wellesley, where there were no men and all the women were reputed to be good-looking, was fifteen miles away.

(Okay, I've used the delusional terms "men" and "women" as long as I can stand. Referring to us as men and women seems as ludicrous now as it then seemed apt then. Harvard officialdom used those terms unfailingly, and we quickly came to bristle at anyone who called us boys and girls. The only people clear-eyed enough to call us that were the townies, for whom "Harvard boy" seemed to be a satisfying pejorative.

We were trying hard to *become* men and women, but we were still seventeen- and eighteen-year-old kids, full of adolescent anxieties and insecurities.)

Early in the term I went to Wellesley to a freshman mixer, surely one of the more barbaric social rituals ever devised by the sophisticates of the East. Some undergraduate organization chartered a bus to carry a load of Harvard boys to Wellesley, where a throng of girls awaited us in a dining hall that had been cleared for dancing.

We all milled around, the boys trying to look cool and detached while frantically trawling for a prospect. Possibly the art of communicating by eye contact hadn't been invented yet; at any rate I can't recall that any of us, boys *or* girls, knew how to do it. Girls stood in groups of three or four pretending to be engrossed in their own conversation and oblivious to the prowling males. As the evening progressed, a few girls could be seen stealing furtive looks around the room, but of course the girls we wanted were those who were able to appear oblivious to the objective of the mixer.

I worked up enough courage to ask a girl to dance. She acted as if she resented having her conversation with her friends interrupted, and said, "Thanks, I don't feel like dancing right now." A few minutes later I saw her dancing with someone else.

My next foray went better. A cute girl with short black hair said, "Okay." Her name was Becky and she gave me a nice smile when the song ended. I didn't have foresight enough to ask her immediately for the next dance, and before I knew it some other guy danced away with her. Now that others had seen her dancing, she was on the floor constantly.

One number during the evening was announced as "ladies' choice." A girl who asked a strange boy to dance any other time would have been thought a harlot, and even at "ladies' choice" girls hoped to be able to ask their favorite partner from earlier in the evening, rather than approach a stranger. As a boy, you hoped that you would turn out to be your favorite's favorite too, and if that didn't happen, you hoped not to be picked by some desperate homely girl. It was as close as we boys ever got to seeing how oppressive the conventions were for a girl.

I had lost sight of Becky and was edging away from a large girl who was beginning to look predatory when someone beside me said, "May I have this dance?" It was Becky, and I was so pleased I must have looked silly. I danced every dance with Becky after that.

By eleven o'clock we boys were back on the bus and I was plotting to get a date with Becky. I would need a car. It was possible, just barely, to get to Wellesley by public bus, but it wouldn't be much of a date if we couldn't go anywhere after I got there.

Renting a car was ridiculously expensive, but I calculated that I could manage it if I could get two friends to split the cost with me. That wasn't easy to arrange. First I had to persuade them that they could afford it and that we would all have a really good time. Then I had to get Becky to line up blind dates for them. We decided that if we were going to spend so much money on a car, we might as well make it a big day—take the our dates to a Harvard football game and then to dinner.

The game was against one of the "C" teams that Harvard always played early in the season—Colgate or Cornell or Columbia, I don't remember which. The three of us picked up the rental car on Saturday morning and somehow found our way through the maze of suburbs to Wellesley. Becky and the two blind dates were waiting at their dormitory.

I had told Becky that my two friends were tall. Apparently she considered nothing else when she picked the girls. One, Louella, was tall and skinny. The other was tall and broad. I think her name was Horatia, but that could be just a mean-spirited invention of my memory. When I saw them I feared that my friends might back out on the spot, but they only gave me dirty looks.

Unaccountably, we had failed to consider how to seat three boys and three girls as couples in a 1957 Oldsmobile. With all four doors open, the six of us stood pondering the issue until one of the girls said, "I guess we'll get in the back." My friends got in the front seat with me, and instantly the car lost all value except as a means of transportation.

By the time we arrived at the stadium no natural affinities had announced themselves, so whose date was Louella and whose Horatia was decided by the accident of seating. It didn't matter, because there wasn't an iota of chemistry among the four of them. It turned out that Louella and Horatia didn't like football, so the two of them chattered about matters inscrutable to the rest of us.

By now it was clear that I would never get my two friends to pitch in on a car rental again, so I was trying to make the most of this apparent last opportunity with Becky. But every time I got a conversation going with her, Louella and Horatia would demand that she comment on one of their trivialities. My efforts at a suave train of patter were repeatedly derailed by their girlish gossip.

We should have cut our losses and taken the girls home after the game, but Harvard had not yet taught us to think strategically, so we carried through with our plan to take them to dinner. We went to a German restaurant in Harvard Square. It was mobbed after the game and we had to wait interminably for a table for six. The girls ordered as if they hadn't eaten for weeks, the bill was astronomical, and it was so late when we finished that there was no time for dalliance before their dormitory curfew.

It was my last Wellesley date until a year or two later, when I had my own car.

The only class in which I did well that first year was the mandatory freshman writing class. A frighteningly self-possessed Radcliffe girl named Stephanie sat near me in that class. The instructor's occasional praise of my essays caused Stephanie to acknowledge my existence, and with that encouragement I asked her to go with me to a play in Boston.

Radcliffe freshmen had early curfews, but they could come home later—midnight, I think—a few times each semester. Stephanie was willing to give me the pleasure of her company for the play, but she wasn't willing to waste one of her "lates" on me. After careful calculation, I assured her we could get back early enough that she wouldn't have to use a late.

Getting to the play required a long walk from her Radcliffe dorm to the Harvard Square station, a trip on the subway to the Park Street station in Boston, and then a trolley ride through Back Bay to Kenmore Square.

When we came out of the theater it was snowing hard. Everything was covered with wet sticky snow and nothing looked familiar. Six streets and three trolley lines intersected at Kenmore Square. Boston's squares were hopelessly confusing to a boy from a place where all roads intersected at right angles. I wasn't entirely sure which trolley we should take; somehow it seemed that we were boarding in a different place from where we had disembarked.

The play had lasted a little longer than I anticipated and Stephanie's curfew was on both our minds. Not wanting to appear so devoid of savoir faire as to be unable to find my way home, I confidently ushered her aboard the first trolley that approached.

The play had been good and I seemed to be hitting it off with Stephanie. The trolley was cozy. Looking out through the snow flakes at the passing cityscape was romantic. At the front of the car a slightly drunk Irishman was amusing the passengers by hanging by his knees from the overhead grab-bar.

After a while I realized he and we were the only people in the car. That was terribly wrong; there should be *more* passengers as we got closer to Park Street, not fewer. I swallowed my savoir faire and asked the driver if we were headed for Park Street.

"Park Street! Not tonight. This car's going to the car barn. There's one more stop. Get off there. I think there should be one more trolley going back toward Park tonight."

Stephanie and I got off and waited in the dark and the snow. There wasn't a person or a car in sight. She didn't say a word. I realized I didn't even know which way to start walking. We waited because we didn't know what else to do. Finally a trolley came, we got back to Park Street and then to Harvard Square, and then ran, into the wind and snow, across Cambridge Common to Radcliffe.

At the dorm Stephanie had to ring for the housemother to let her in. She slipped quickly in the door without a word to me. As I stood in the snow on the doorstep and watched the door close, I heard her explaining that her date had taken her the wrong way on the trolley. Of course that was my only date with Stephanie.

Since then I've thought less often of her than of the drunken Irishman, who was still hanging upside down on the outbound trolley when it pulled away from the last stop. Did the driver leave him aboard when he put the trolley away for the night in the car barn?

The rest of the year was a long slow test of test of psychological endurance. I didn't admit defeat, but I didn't feel exactly triumphant either. I turned my amorous attentions to my girlfriend back home. I toughed out my courses, and was grateful, if embarrassed, to escape from French with a D.

When finals were over I hitchhiked home, deliriously happy to be leaving Harvard and the East behind. The first morning after I got home I saddled Jack and rode down in the Platte River bottoms. The river was full from the spring thaw in the mountains, beaver were busy building new dams, wildflowers were in bloom, and young calves were frolicking, tails pointed at the sky, running and bucking in ever-widening orbits from their mothers. The air was sweet with the smell of wild roses. After a year of city smells, I realized what a perfect scent that is.

That summer I got a job as a wrangler in Colorado, guiding dudes on trail rides and camping trips in the mountains. It was the best job I ever had—a summer of horses, girls, fresh air, and splendid scenery.

When fall came I couldn't face going back to Harvard, so I worked for a year as a reporter for the *North Platte Telegraph-Bulletin*. That paper happened to be run by a superb editor, Keith Blackledge, who quickly threw me into the exciting and very adult world of news. In that year of independence and self-sufficiency, my sense of self stopped taking the shape of whatever vessel it found itself in. When I returned to Harvard the next year, I was able to absorb the experience without letting it dissolve my connection to my previous life.

[24]

Home Isn't There Anymore

TWENTY-FIVE YEARS after my family moved away from Union, I took my daughter, Elizabeth, to see where I had grown up. She was ten or twelve, not quite old enough to automatically recoil from everything parental. She was a city girl, for whom childhood was a structured thing, generally supervised by adults. I was eager for her to see how different my childhood had been, twenty-five years earlier. I planned to show her the one-room school, the grove where I found a newborn colt on my tenth birthday, the corrals where I broke him to ride, the canal where I trapped muskrats, the canyons where we hunted coyotes.

We drove south from Gothenburg, crossed the Platte River, then turned west and began to zig-zag northwestward up the valley toward Union. I wasn't surprised to see that the road for the first few miles was now paved; you expect some things to change in a quarter century. Soon the pavement gave way to the gravel I remembered.

In the Platte Valley the roads all run north-south or east-west and there is one on every side of each square mile. Until you get close to your destination, it really doesn't matter what route you take because the hills south of the valley deflect you to the right and the river deflects you to the left, just as they did for the wagon trains on the Oregon Trail.

I was full of gratitude to Elizabeth for indulging me this outing, and I was so absorbed in talking with her that I hadn't paid much attention to the surroundings. When I realized we should be getting close to Union, I tried to get my bearings. Suddenly I had the feeling that I must have taken a very wrong turn. I recognized nothing. It

houses had replaced the homely old frame
nal steel building had replaced a weathered
at I had expected. Instead, most of the old things
literated.

remembered had been a peopled place, farmsteads
by groves of trees, a mailbox and a driveway along the
y half-mile or so. The pattern of settlement had been farms
rter-section each, because 160 acres had been the unit a settler
claim under the laws that parceled out the plains—the Pre-
ption Act, the Homestead Act, and the Timber Culture Act. There
had been some consolidation by the middle of the twentieth century,
but several farms per section was still the norm. When a farmer who
had survived the drought or the hard times took over the neighboring
quarter from one who hadn't, the survivor's son or hired man or renter
often occupied the extra house.

In the place of my boyhood, every inch of land testified to human
effort. Fences and cross-fences carved the farms into smaller fields
and pastures, dotted with windmills and haystacks. Each farmhouse
was surrounded by barns, granaries, chicken houses, corn cribs, and
corrals. Most farms had a windbreak—a wide band of trees along the
north side, planted to slow the winter wind and capture snow for the
benefit of the adjoining fields to the south.

The section-line roads were graded a foot or so higher than the
surrounding land so the wind would keep them clear of snow. The
roadside ditches created by this grading were deep and steep, filled
with ten-foot-tall sunflowers, wild roses, and plum thickets. The most
common "auto accident" occurred when one car, meeting another,
veered too far to the right and got pulled by the soft shoulder into one
of these ditches. A farmer with a tractor and a log chain usually could
get the traveler back on the road with only a few scrapes on the side of
the car and a few sunflowers caught in the bumpers.

The land my daughter and I found ourselves in was an empty
place. It wasn't abandoned—far from it. It was intensely farmed, but
as if by an unseen race of giants. The puny creations of mortals—the
houses and barns, the fences, the windbreaks—had been bulldozed

away to create huge fields that stretched away in straight furrows toward a treeless infinity. A few people still lived there, even a few with names I recognized, but they lived in lonely houses standing naked on the plains, houses without windbreaks or barns or windmills. Even the road ditches were gone, graded flat so the furrows could come right to the edge of the road. Many of the roads looked like they were no longer public, just paths to get the invisible giants into their fields.

I gave up trying to get my bearings from the roads and farmsteads and groves of my memory, and began looking for natural landmarks. Surely I could find the gulch that had carved its way through our milk-cow pasture. In winter I had tried to ski on its steep banks and in summer we had sat on the rim in the dark and listened to the roar of floodwaters that nearly washed out the bridge. But I drove across it three times before I recognized it. It too had been bulldozed out of existence, filled and graded and plowed until it was now only a gentle swale in the great field that had swallowed up our farm.

Once I found the vestige of the gulch, I could tell exactly where our house and barns and corrals had been. They were gone, of course, but I felt sure I could find some sign of them—the well, a foundation, some shards of broken glass—or at the very least, a spot in the field where the corn grew a little greener and taller because of the decades of manure that livestock had deposited in our corrals.

I was wrong; there were no artifacts of human habitation. Apparently the fertilizers introduced by agribusiness were so potent they overwhelmed any lingering effects of organic fertilizer. It was as if the land itself had been transformed, from something life-connected to something purely chemical.

We did find one artifact, the old school, but I soon wished we hadn't. It had been moved a mile or two, relieved of the sign that had identified it as Lincoln County School District 74, deprived of the big cast iron bell that had summoned kids across the valley on frosty mornings, and stripped of its blackboards, well-worn pine flooring, and ink-stained desks,. It had been converted to a cattle shed, dumped on uneven ground without a foundation or floor, its once crisp angles now twisting in the early stages of terminal unsteadiness. Now it had ceased to serve even as a cattle shed. There appeared to be no longer any cattle, or any places for cattle, in the valley.

I felt the way you feel when you learn that someone you love has been killed—not just an emotion but a physical sensation, as if you've been hit and knocked silly, an emptiness that forms in your stomach and grows into disbelief, and then anger, and then futility when you realize there isn't a murderer or a drunk driver to hate. I was stunned at the intensity of my reaction; I hadn't realized how much the place mattered to me.

Only the feel of the place remained—the vastness of the sky, the eternal wind, the merciless summer sun, the long view to the brooding hills on the south, the distant tree line guarding the river on the north, the constant motion of the landscape. When I stepped into the narrow shade of the old school building, the dry wind instantly began evaporating the sweat from my body. That delicious chill always gives me a thrill, alerting every nerve in my body that I'm home. Cowley was right: we carry each of us an urn of native soil, "cool and sweet enough to sink the nostrils in, and find the smell of home. . . ."

On the trip back to town I kept thinking of a song that had been popular in the 1950s about a desert settlement in the West that had vanished, buried now by the "shifting, whispering sands." As a community, we too had vanished. What once had been the only world that mattered to me and my family and our neighbors was gone, covered not by sand but agribusiness.

*A few years ago I took this photo
of the corrals where we worked
our cattle—the only visible
remnant our life 60 years earlier.*

[25]

The End of Life on the Land

NOW THIRTY-FIVE MORE YEARS HAVE PASSED since my pilgrimage to Union with my daughter, the trip that bludgeoned me with the realization that the community had vanished. The life I've lived since I left Nebraska has been richer than I could ever have imagined. After graduating from Harvard, I became a newspaperman and covered presidential campaigns, political conventions, and space flights. After that I went to law school, became a law professor, wrote books, and was paid extravagantly for my legal advice. I have friends who are novelists, screenwriters, members of Parliament, and Knights of the Realm. I've seen the Bolshoi ballet in Moscow, the opera in Vienna, and the choir at St. Martin's in the Fields. I've lived in New York, London, and Sydney, dined with ambassadors, chatted with the Queen of England, and lectured in Sweden, Italy, and the Netherlands.

But when my mind is free to wander, it doesn't dwell on those adult experiences. Instead, it revisits the homely magic of neighborhood talent shows at Union School, the distant howling of coyotes on frozen winter nights, the desperate bawling of newly weaned calves, the agony of not having a horse and the ecstasy of finally getting one, the glory of winning a silver dollar at the rodeo, our sometimes peculiar neighbors—and always, the warm enveloping arms of a community in which everyone was needy, but also needed.

I'm still trying to understand why Union meant so much to me. I've talked about it with childhood friends, my siblings and parents, and a couple of my early teachers, and found that memories of Union have an unaccountably strong grip on them too.

By any objective measure, it was not a time and place to envy. For most of us, financial distress was one hailstorm away. Health care was minimal; we saw the doctor only when we had a broken bone or something more serious than mumps or measles, and we visited the dentist only when we had a toothache. A fire truck or ambulance was at least half an hour away in good weather, nonexistent when roads were impassable. We had no indoor plumbing, and our water came from shallow wells surrounded by corrals full of livestock filth. We slept in unheated bedrooms, controlled mice with cheese-loaded traps, combated flies with strips of flypaper hung from the ceiling, and induced moths to drown themselves in a pan of kerosene held under a bright light. The climate was brutal, violent death was frequent, and isolation was our only constant companion.

So why were we so fond of Union? One answer, of course, is that everyone's childhood is special. The child's mind is virgin soil; first experiences stick; early impressions remain vivid long after later ones have faded. My aged grandfather could reach back seventy-five years to his boyhood in Sweden after he could no longer remember what he ate for breakfast. And of course nostalgia is a powerful filter, excising unhappiness and leaving a stronger concoction of pleasant memories.

Also, Union's legacy was protected by its early death. The community vanished quickly, disappearing before we had to watch it decline. Like John Kennedy, James Dean, and Buddy Holly, it is fixed in memory at its vibrant best, leaving an image unclouded by overexposure, aging, or anticlimax. In my childhood it seemed not only healthy but immortal, and by the time I came back to check on it, it was gone.

I now understand some of the reasons for its demise. The first mortal wound to Union and its way of life was delivered by prosperity. The 1940s were good years for farming on the plains, maybe the best ever. The rains came. First the war, and then the post-war boom, kept crop and livestock prices high. Irrigation and mechanization, which had begun before the war, now exploded. There were no restrictions on pumping ground water, so farmers leveled their fields and drilled wells. At first they irrigated only to help the crops through dry spells, then they learned that with enough water and fertilizer you can produce more, year in and year out, than rainfall yields even in the best years. Tractors replaced horses in the late thirties and early forties, and the first generation of crude, simple tractors was replaced after the war by big, powerful, versatile ones that could work twice as much land.

Farmers and ranchers were no longer subsisting—they were making money. By the 1950s, we didn't have to borrow equipment from our neighbors. We bought what we needed, and they did too. Once we could afford hired men, we didn't need the help of our neighbors very often. We could stay overnight at the grandparents' without having to arrange for a neighbor to feed and water the livestock evening and morning. We still worked together for branding, but other communal jobs, like threshing and corn shelling, disappeared because John Deere and International Harvester developed machines that threshed the wheat and shelled the corn as they harvested it.

My family bought our first new car, a '48 Dodge, and we took our first vacation in the summer of 1949. My parents left my sisters with Cora Jacox, the neighborhood spinster, and took me on the annual Nebraska Hereford Tour. We visited the big ranches of Hereford breeders in the Sandhills. One of those belonged to former Nebraska governor Sam McKelvie, who had the only paved driveway any of us had ever seen.

The first night my parents and I slept on the ground at Chadron State Park, the three of us cocooned in an old bed tarp from Dad's days as a ranch hand in Montana. In the middle of the night a rainstorm hit. After trying for a while to keep the water out of the tarp, we gave up and drove into Chadron, where we spent the rest of the night sleeping in chairs in the lobby of an old hotel.

The next day we drove across the Pine Ridge Reservation in South Dakota and picked up some hitchhikers, a young Sioux couple (a brave and a squaw, as Dad said). The couple invited us to go with them to an Indian rodeo near a tiny reservation town called Oglala. Most of the Indians had come in horse-drawn wagons. Hundreds of wagons and a few old cars and trucks were parked in a circle that must have been a quarter-mile across. It was like an opening scene from a cowboy-and-Indian movie—hundreds of Indians scattered across the plains under an endless sky, few sounds except the wind, little motion except for the undulating grass. Every ten minutes or so, somewhere in the circle an Indian would climb on a wild horse and try to ride it.

We watched for a while, then drove on to the Black Hills and Mount Rushmore and the Cave of the Winds. I don't think we were away from home more than two nights, but it seemed like we had been around the world.

The county improved the roads. People quit shopping in Brady and went instead to Gothenburg or North Platte, where there were restaurants and real movie theaters. A woman named Nettie Jean, the object of much gossip because she wore a leotard and lots of makeup, came from North Platte once a week and gave dance lessons in Gothenburg, teaching young people the bop, the tango, the cha-cha-cha, and the fox-trot. Some people went once or twice a year to Omaha or Denver and came home with the kind of women's clothes they saw in the magazines. A few built summer cabins around Jeffrey Lake and bought fishing boats with outboard motors. An evening of card-playing or Sunday dinner at the neighbors' was no longer a satisfying entertainment.

As prosperity always does, it blessed some and skipped others. There were hired men who died still working for someone else, and tenants who never owned their own land, and others, like Clarence and Mabel Peterson, who eventually became landowners but had to leave the community to do it. So not everybody was buying new cars, taking vacations, and building lakeside cabins. But enough people prospered that it changed the community.

In the early '50s television came to our part of the world. The station was a hundred miles away, in Hastings, and we couldn't pull in its signal at all until the station built a retransmission tower a mere forty miles away. But even if the picture was barely visible through the snow, watching the Army-McCarthy hearings and Doris Day took the place of evenings with neighbors.

Still, the community might have survived if the school had. But the school too was a victim of rising expectations. The problem was high school. There was a school bus from Brady, but it didn't come as far as Union. In earlier years, kids who wanted to go on to high school after finishing the eighth grade at Union usually boarded in town with relatives during the week, returning home for weekends and school vacations. But as the roads improved and families could afford a second vehicle, students sometimes drove themselves to high school in town, and their younger siblings transferred to town school too because they could ride with the eldest. When this became common, loyalties to country school began to crack.

The Tetros were the first of our neighbors to abandon Union altogether. When Joe was about ready for ninth grade, they built a house just outside Brady. It was the first ranch-style house in our part of the valley and was rumored to have cost $30,000. "You'd need roller skates just to get from one end to the other," people said. When the Tetros moved to town, Union lost not only Joe but also his three younger sisters. A couple of years later, when I was ready for high school, our move to the farm near Gothenburg took my three sisters out of Union too.

The school survived for four more years, and it wasn't the departure of the Tetros and Andersons that killed it. New kids moved in to take our places, and when the school closed it had fourteen pupils, about the same as it always had. But our departure revealed the fatal truth: parents would take their children out of Union if they could. I don't think they were seriously dissatisfied with the quality of education at Union—in any event, the elementary schools in Brady and Gothenburg didn't have educational ambitions much grander than Union's. What turned the parents' heads was the prospect of a richer extracurricular life.

The Brady school board built a new gymnasium and music facilities, and then held a meeting at Union and persuaded the parents that their children needed to get started in band and basketball before they entered high school. I doubt that it was a hard sell; once parents began to envision futures for their children away from Union, it was natural to assume that town schools were more suitable for kids destined for life in towns.

Closing the country schools encouraged families to move to town.

It was no harder for the farmer to commute from town to the farm than for the kids to commute from the farm to town. Soon there were more farmers living in town than on the land.

It was a time of extraordinary social mobility. In 1940 my father was a hired hand with nothing but a wife, a baby, and a few cows. By 1950 we owned a thousand acres and had our own hired man. In 1952 I was the only kid in my class at a one-room country school without indoor plumbing; in 1957 I was a freshman at Harvard College.

Prosperity made these changes possible, but it isn't the whole story. Prosperity only allowed people to do what they apparently had wanted to do all along. Farmers could have put their new wealth in the bank instead of buying machinery, but apparently they weren't so fond of sharing machinery after all. If you bought your own, you didn't have to wait while the ideal time to plant corn passed you by, or worry that a hailstorm might come before you were able to borrow the neighbor's combine to harvest your wheat.

If people had really cherished the social life of the community, they wouldn't have had to give it up for television and trips to the city. Couples who used to play cards together could have switched to watching television together. Families could have taken their trips with the people they used to have Sunday dinner with. But they didn't. Instead they adopted a lifestyle like that of the rest of America, a style that traded neighborliness for individual freedom.

My guess is that people let the community slip away without realizing it was happening. They bought machinery because they could afford it, not considering how their relations with neighbors would change when they no longer needed to share. They watched television because it was novel and everybody was watching it, not understanding how it would alter social interaction. They sent their kids to town schools for the advantages those offered, not calculating the costs of losing the community school. If they appreciated the aggregate effects of these individual choices, they did so too late, after the point of no return had passed.

The outside world was changing too. A growing economy, receding social barriers, contraception, air travel, and accessible higher education offered temptations that were hard to resist. For me, the seduction began with a train trip to the east coast, which opened my eyes to a more exciting and glamorous world. My contemporaries had their own eye-openers—college, military service, or jobs as secretaries and airline stewardesses. Denver, Omaha, Kansas City, and many smaller cities are full of farm kids who left home to see the bright lights and never returned. More of my childhood friends now live in California and Texas than live in Brady and Gothenburg.

The rural communities are gone, and so is life on the land. The plains are still populated, of course. Most of the towns survive. The land is still owned and farmed, but now it belongs mostly to people who use it as the Indians did: they harvest its bounty, but they make their permanent settlements in more hospitable locales. Living in town off the proceeds of the land isn't life on the land. If settlement means physical occupation by people who live on the land in settled communities, that has pretty much ended. It lasted less than a hundred years.

Epilogue

AFTER I HAD WRITTEN THIS MEMOIR, and while it was in my computer waiting to be turned into something publishable, Joe
Tetro published his own memoir. Joe was three when I was born on
the Tetro ranch, and for the first ten years of my life Joe was my best
friend. At Union School, Joe was my hero, the older boy whose lead
I followed—into mischief, adventure, and possibly even learning.
Until the Tetros moved into town when I was ten, we shared the same
teachers, schoolmates, neighbors, brandings, Christmas programs,
pie socials, chivarees, and foolish pranks.

Joe's book is called *Lost in America: Memoirs of a Maverick*. It's
a powerful, high-energy account of an extraordinary life—of ram-
bling across America and Europe, of dumpster-diving and hitch-hik-
ing, of time in mental hospitals both as patient and worker, of copious
amounts of alcohol and sex, of brawling and anger and hurt, but also of
tenderness and love. Two-thirds of it is about his adult life. He worked
on a railroad section gang and as a fruit picker, learned Russian in
the Army, drank and womanized his way through a tour of duty in
Germany, and joined up with a congenial set of misfits at the University
of Nebraska. Then it was California, encounter groups, lots of wine
and weed, playing guitar in parks and clubs, a job at a state mental
hospital, and eventually into hospitalization himself. Finally, he ini-
tiated a correspondence with a woman in the Philippines, flew to
Hong Kong and married her, and brought her back to California. The
marriage has lasted more than 30 years and seems to have made it
possible for Joe to channel his demons into his well-written memoir
and hundreds of poems, some of them very lovely.

The first chapters of Joe's book are about his childhood. He tells of many of the same events and people that I have described in this book—the rodeos, the roundups and brandings, the 4-H meetings, the teachers and neighbors. But for all the intertwining, his account is very different from mine. He recalls that all the boys at Union once collaborated for weeks to build a pyramid of feces on the seat of the boys' outhouse—a project I don't remember at all. He doesn't remember the infamous horse-turd fight that took place at his ranch during the 4-H Club meeting.

I'm not surprised that our recollections often differ—people remember different things, and remember the same things differently. But it's not just that our memories of specific events differ. The childhood I remember is a happy one. The childhood he depicts is one filled with pain, fear, and anger. His father was cruel, demanding, unforgiving, and abusive—sometimes physically, often verbally. His mother was alcoholic and sometimes suicidal. His sister Terre was mistreated even worse than he was. The neighbors that I found congenial and reassuring, he found hypocritical. The mother of the five-year-old that I wooed too persistently remonstrated only mildly with me, but flew into an uncontrolled rage at Joe when he affronted her older daughter. I thought the Tetros were admired by their neighbors: Joe thought they were envied. The community that seemed friendly and empowering to me seemed hostile and constricting to him. He found the culture of our time and place oppressive; I found it supportive.

At first I wondered if I had been deluding myself all these years, cultivating a mythical happy childhood while repressing memories of pain and unhappiness. I don't think that's the case. I do have unhappy memories, such as hating school at Maywood and being horseless at roundup time, and those are as vivid as the happy ones. But the unhappy times were few and the happy ones were many. My boyhood experience really was far different from Joe's.

My blind spot was in not seeing that it wasn't the same for all of us. I was oblivious to Joe's pain. I didn't realize he suffered from asthma. I didn't know about the times his mother was sent off to a psychiatric hospital, or the times his father knocked him across the corral. Nor did

I remember that he was as voracious a reader as I, or that he was at least as bright. He was just my older friend, the one who always had a horse, the one who got to do things I was told I was too young to do. I didn't see that beneath his bravado was a delicate, vulnerable psyche.

Sadly, others didn't see that either. Since Joe's book came out, he and I have maintained a regular correspondence, and we've tried to understand why our impressions are so different. I've asked him whether he thinks anyone understood him during his years at Union, and his answer is no. That disappoints me greatly, because Esther Atkinson, who taught both of us for three years, was Joe's mother's best friend. I thought Esther understood each of us; she of all people should have known of the dysfunction in Joe's family and should have appreciated its effects on Joe. If she didn't, that may be some evidence that Joe's view of our community is true. But mine is true too; mine is the view of a boy from a happy family, with loving parents whose nurture made their children as confident and secure as Joe's made him fearful and hurt.

Reconnecting with Joe after more than fifty years has been one of the highlights of my life. Joe graduated from Union School and moved to town when he was thirteen and I was ten. I don't recall ever seeing him again. Our lives since then have been very different. But when we began corresponding after his book came out, old affections poured out like tears from a long-suppressed sorrow.

We exchange emails every few days. We compare memories about that long-ago place and its people, of course, but we share far more than reminiscences. We're both admirers of David Riesman, the great sociologist of the twentieth century—I because he was one of my favorite professors at Harvard, Joe because Riesman's *The Lonely Crowd* spoke to him about the alienation of the individual in modern society. Joe introduced me to the novels of Gerald Green and James Agee, and I rekindled Joe's appreciation of Wallace Stegner. Joe gave me his father's chaps, custom-made from elk hide in 1925 by a storied Denver saddle maker; I have them on display beside my dad's saddle from the 1930s. It's as if our souls were programmed—there in the wind and dust and snow and drudgery—with a bond too strong to be broken by mere time and distance.

Our little clutch of interdependent families in the far corner of Lincoln County is now remembered in two memoirs. I think I understand how they can be so different. It's because a vanished community exists only in the hearts of those it nurtured or wounded, and is remembered accordingly.